Bible Basics Youth Electives

God

The Awesome Almighty

Paul Woods, Editor

David C. Cook Publishing Co.

Elgin, Illinois—Weston, Ontario

This youth elective was developed through the combined efforts and resources of a number of David C. Cook's dedicated lesson writers. It was compiled and edited by Paul Woods and designed by Christopher Patchel and Jean Warfel, with cover design by Russ Peterson. Cover photo by Bakstad Photographics.

GOD
The Awesome Almighty

© 1988 David C. Cook Publishing Co.

Scripture quotations are from the Holy Bible: New International Version (NIV), © 1973, 1978, 1984 by the New York International Bible Society. Used by permission of Zondervan Bible Publishers.

Published by David C. Cook Publishing Co.
850 N. Grove Ave., Elgin, IL 60120
Cable address: DCCOOK
Printed in U.S.A.

ISBN: 1-55513-873-X

CONTENTS

GOD: THE AWESOME ALMIGHTY

Every year, more than 30,000 books are published in the U.S. alone. Every hour, thousands of radio newscasts send "vital" information to millions of listeners. Every minute, 24 hours a day, anyone with a telephone can dial recorded public service messages about dozens of subjects ranging from AIDS to the weather.

Information about nearly every subject from sex to superconductors is available to kids via the library, school, TV or computer hookup. So much data is available, in fact, that we're said to be in the middle of an Information Explosion.

Despite all the flying facts and figures, however, society is mostly silent when it comes to discussing God. Theologians are dismissed as the ultimate Trivial Pursuers, nitpickers who ought to quit arguing and do something "useful." God is assumed to be nonexistent or at best unknowable, with each person's guess as good as anyone else's. The result is that many people, kids and adults, create their own little gods as the need arises.

These mini-gods are usually comforting, powerless, unobtrusive. Their makers are highly offended when someone claims to know "the one, true God," for god-making is supposed to be a very private matter. It is so private, in fact, that God is the only Person too controversial to be discussed in the classroom or the courtroom.

In such an atmosphere, is it any wonder that most kids grow up as strangers to the God of the Bible?

Even Christian young people, like their elders, often harbor misconceptions about the Almighty. They may see Him as impersonal, disinterested, aloof; cruel, capricious, untrustworthy; or so forgiving and warmhearted that He couldn't bear to say no to our self-indulgence.

As a leader, you have the opportunity to help your teens discover the Biblical God. This course will help. You'll begin with a reassuring discussion of God's existence. In successive sessions, you'll examine many of God's characteristics, including His triune nature, His power, His love, His dependability, and His desire to mercifully correct us.

But you won't stop there. Each session will help your students *respond* to what they've discovered about

God. The result can be significant spiritual growth as well as knowledge.

Our society may be content with an unknown God, but *you* don't have to be. As you lead young people through these sessions, may you and they come to know the one, true God more intimately than ever before.

About the Bible Basics Youth Electives Series

Young people need firm foundations. Social events, games, and opinion-sharing discussions, good as they are, can't replace solid Bible learning. Whether that learning takes place in Sunday School, an evening Bible study, or another setting, it *must* be Bible-based and Christ-centered in order to give kids the timeless answers they need.

That's where Bible Basics Youth Electives come in. These 13-session courses allow your teens to spend time studying vital Scriptural truths *in depth*. The session plans provide you with background, questions and answers, and life response suggestions that will help you lead productive learning times.

Clear goals are stated for each three-step session, along with key verses and a list of the few items you'll need.

You'll rarely need more than Bibles, pencils, paper, a chalkboard or flip chart, and copies of the reproducible student Action Sheets in the back of this book. There are no student manuals to buy; just make enough copies of the Action Sheets for your students and visitors.

You'll find the sessions easy to follow. Instructions to the leader are in regular type; things you might say directly to students are in bold type. Plenty of material for 45- to 60-minute sessions is included; feel free to adapt the plans to fit your time and group.

May God use His Word to build firm foundations in the lives of your young people—and to strengthen your own as well.

IS ANYBODY THERE?

Session Aim

That your students' faith in God will be strengthened by an examination of creation and God's eternal nature.

Key Verse

"By faith we understand that the universe was formed at God's command, so that what is seen was not made out of what was visible" (Hebrews 11:3).

Things You'll Need

- *Pencils*
- *Bibles*
- *"Know God or No God?" (Action Sheet 1A)*
- *"God Is!" (Action Sheet 1B)*

***Atheists say God doesn't exist.** Agnostics say that even if He does exist, we can't know Him. Some scientists claim that the Bible, from which we draw most of our conclusions about God, is fiction—a fairy tale that has little to do with scientific reality.*

What effect do these people have on the Christian teenager? They can create serious doubts in even the most committed kids.

This session will help your students understand that the God of the Bible is not a fairy-tale character. Kids will see that God is the Creator of the universe, the One who is still in control—the One who is not surprised or threatened by scientific discoveries. Your kids' faith will grow as they better understand who God is and learn how to explain their belief in Him to kids who have questions.

1

CRITICS' CORNER

Goal: That your students will consider how rational it is to believe in God's existence.

Begin your class by asking the following question: **How do we know God exists?**

Let kids respond. Encourage them to give you several proofs. When they run out of ideas, let them know that the existence of God is your topic for today's session. Then begin the following activity.

Divide your class into three groups, even if you only have three kids. Cut apart the three statements on "Know God or No God?" (Action Sheet 1A) and give one to each group. Have kids study the statement on their group's sheet and decide how to argue against it or demonstrate its weakness. They should be ready to support their position by supplying at least one logical explanation or one example from their experience. Have each group present its responses for the rest of the class. Here are the statements and possible responses:

A. A Soviet cosmonaut claimed that on his trip into space he could not see God; therefore, God must not exist.

(According to that logic, if you don't see something then it must not exist. But doesn't the wind exist? Scripture says that God is a Spirit, and a spirit can't be seen. Many things in life really exist even though we don't see them.)

B. I can't accept the existence of God on faith. Faith is unscientific.

(Aren't there some things you accept on faith? What about love, friendship, instructions in a cookbook? Even scientists use faith. A scientist puts faith in a theory because he believes that his interpretation of the evidence is true.)

C. It's only a matter of time until people know all the answers. Scientists will eventually explain the universe without having to give God any credit.

(Some questions will never be answered by scientists. People can't see how things began, nor can they tell how things will turn out. They can't gather enough hard evidence to "prove" the past or the future. They can come up with theories, but sooner or later they run out of evidence.)

After your kids give their responses, paraphrase the following:

How do we know for sure what the creation around us tells us? Do we cram pebbles under a microscope and look for God's pulse? No, we make intelligent use of the evidence. One kind of evidence we'll examine today is the evidence from Scripture.

2 FOR THE RECORD

Goal: That your students will record evidence from Scripture that shows God can be recognized in nature.

The Scriptures you'll look at in this session illustrate for kids that we can not only know that God exists, but that we can know what He is like.

Pass out copies of "God Is!" (Action Sheet 1B), and have your kids read the introduction. Then have kids work through parts 1 and 2 on their own. Go over each part as your kids finish it.

God Is!

A Bible study on Genesis 1:1; Exodus 3:13-15; Romans 1:19, 20; Hebrews 11:3.

1. Begin today's study by going through all the passages listed above as if you didn't know anything except what these Scriptures tell you about God. Then list all His characteristics which you can know for certain or which are implied in these verses.

Circle those on your list that are specifically stated, and be prepared to tell why you included the others. For example, in Genesis 1:1, you could circle the fact that God is the Creator.

You might also put on your list that He is eternal because this is implied. You can assume that if God was present in the beginning, He Himself had no beginning.

(God is Creator of the world. He is eternal. God claims to be "I Am Who I Am." The God who created the world is the same One who speaks to man. God reveals His invisible qualities—such as eternal power—through His creation. God created the world out of nothing with a simple command. He is all-powerful.)

What do you think the expression, "I AM THAT I AM" told Moses about God?

(God is beyond explanation. He has always been. He is there and needs no proof.)

Read or summarize the following information.

God's answer sounds strange to us: "I AM THAT I AM." But that's because our language has no way of translating what the Hebrew word meant, although even in the Hebrew word there is a sense of mystery. The very "am" is an indefinite tense—its meaning includes "I am" and "I will be." God is past, present and future. He has neither beginning nor end.

Moses and the other Hebrew people believed in one God, but they had been living for 400 years in a land where people worshiped many different gods. Israel's God was not like the snakes, frogs, and bulls which Egypt worshiped. He was indescribable and above total explanation.

2. Reread Romans 1:19, 20. Below write a brief note to an imaginary or real friend, explaining how God can be seen through creation.

(Answers will vary, but here is one possibility:

Dear friend,
God lets us know that He is there. One way He does it is through His creation. For example, we can see that God's power reaches over huge distances; just look at the stars and galaxies in space and the gigantic oceans on earth. The order of our solar system shows God's wisdom. Our planet works together with the sun and moon to provide us with a variety of climates and seasons. God's care for His creation can be seen in the natural and amazing instincts of wild animals, birds, and reptiles.)

If a non-Christian begins looking at nature honestly, he or she can understand that a being beyond himself or herself did the creating. But no one could ever totally discover God and develop a friendship with Him just by looking at God's creation.

Through creation a person can come to the conclusion that there is a God and he or she doesn't know this God. But nature can't save that person from a life of separation from God.

God didn't allow the stars, trees, and green grass to communicate His salvation message. He allows them to be pointers and gave the job of communicating His salvation mes-

sage to His followers, through His Word.

If creation shows us God's perfect nature, how do you account for the fact that in creation we see killing, decay, and death?

(Have kids look up Romans 8:19-23. This passage describes how nature, like mankind, has been subjected to the bondage of decay, and is suffering under it. Creation was perfect when God created it. But like mankind, creation is fallen and the evil aspects we see are an expression of that fallen state. But even though creation is fallen, we can catch glimpses of God's goodness and perfection through its beauty.)

Have your kids go over number 3 on the "God Is" sheet in pairs.

3. Think back over the Scriptures you've studied today. What verse would be the best evidence to give someone who refuses to believe there is a God? Explain your choice to one other person in the room.

(Kids' answers will vary.)

Logic and nature can lead a person toward the conclusion that God exists. But faith must take one across the final step to accepting the conclusion as a personal belief. We must have faith to "see" that there is a Creator God. Our Key Verse points that out.

Have your kids read Hebrews 11:3 and put it in their own words. Have volunteers tell how they would say it.

The basic concept here is that God made nature out of nothing. Hence, God is the source of all life.

3 THE GOD WHO IS

Goal: That your students will give praise to God for having revealed Himself to us through creation.

The Bible is not a science textbook. But we can believe what it says about scientific things. It doesn't claim to make "scientific" statements; it does claim to make true statements. Science changes as people gain more knowledge. If the Bible ever seems to disagree with scientific information, we must question that scientific information and also check to make certain we are not misunderstanding the language of the Bible.

Have your kids look at section 4 on the "God Is" sheet. This section will require your kids to think through and use all they've learned in this session. Verbalizing what they've thought about will help establish these truths more firmly in kids' minds.

Break your group into pairs, and assign one roleplay to each pair. Give kids a few minutes to think and talk through what they want to do, then have the pairs present their roleplays for the rest of the class.

4. Roleplay one of the following:

A. How would a Christian use the Scripture studied today and all the other information he or she knows to explain God's existence to a friend who doesn't believe that God exists?

B. A friend tells a Christian that he or she might have believed in God before we began to conquer space. But now humans have done so many things that people used to think only God could do. So the friend refuses to believe that there is a God.

After each roleplay is presented, let your class discuss the points that were brought out. Don't let anyone's arguments be ridiculed. Encourage your kids to remember the things you've discussed to help them when their faith in God is challenged.

What effect has today's discussion had on your faith in God?

(Give your kids a minute to reflect, and then try to get each one to respond. Some, at least, will probably say that their faith has become stronger.)

How will the things we've learned help you tomorrow or next week?

(Again, give all your kids a chance to respond.)

Conclude your session with a praise circle, giving your kids an opportunity to praise God for revealing Himself in creation.

Form a circle and have all those who want to praise God for something in creation do so. You might want to give your kids the following structure in which they can give their praise: "Thank You, Lord, for creating (tall trees); this shows me that You (like beauty and strength)." Let kids pray as many times as they wish.

Try ending your prayer time with Psalm 104:24, 33, 34:

"How many are your works, O Lord! In wisdom you made them all; the earth is full of your creatures. I will sing to the Lord all my life; I will sing praise to my God as long as I live. May my meditation be pleasing to him, as I rejoice in the Lord."

A MYSTERY THAT MATTERS

Session Aim

That your students will begin to comprehend why the doctrine of the Trinity is important.

Key Verse

"Before me no god was formed, nor will there be one after me. I, even I, am the Lord, and apart from me there is no savior" (Isaiah 43:10b, 11).

Things You'll Need

● *"Our Three-in-One God" (Action Sheet 2A)*
● *"Like God or Not?" (Action Sheet 2B)*
● *Bibles, pencils, paper*

How can one God be three at the same time?

Everyone has trouble understanding that mystery, and teenagers are no exception. And why should they care? Because the doctrine of the Trinity is one that is at the basis of the Christian faith.

This session looks at both sides of the issue: the oneness of God and the threeness of God. Is there really just one God? Or is Christianity like religions that have many gods? From the Scriptures they examine in this session, your kids will begin to understand and appreciate the importance of the Trinity.

1 WHO IS YOUR GOD?

Goal: That your students will see why it is important to understand as much as we can about God.

Let's say someone who knows nothing about Christianity asks you, "Who is this God you worship? What makes Him different from the gods of other religions?" How would you explain our God to this person? Think of a one-sentence description of the way God is, and use it to complete the sentence, "God is . . ."

Give paper and pencils to your students and have them complete the sentence. Tell kids not to put their names on their papers. When they finish, collect all the definitions and read them aloud. Ask: **Does it matter what we think God is like? Why?** Allow kids to offer answers if they wish. Then, using lecture or discussion, give them the following information:

You may think it's less important to understand God than it is to know Him personally through Jesus. It *is* more important to be close to God than it is to just talk about what He's like. But in a way your relationship with God is like one you develop with a friend. The more you learn about your friend's personality, ideas, and background, the closer your relationship can become.

Theology is the study of God and His message. We look at theology to learn certain things about God, not as a substitute for experiencing Him.

What can theology teach us? First, it can teach us which god to worship. There are many different, often conflicting ideas about God floating around these days. How are you going to know which to follow? Also, theology can teach us how to live our daily lives. The way we think about God will affect how we behave toward our friends (and enemies), how we think of ourselves, how we pray, and whether we honor God with our actions. It will determine what kind of persons we become. So we need to get as clear an idea as we can of what God is like.

Some gods are easy to understand. The Greek gods, for instance, were thought to be just like Greek men and women, only better. Were Greek men strong? The gods were superstrong! Were Greek women beautiful? The goddesses were stunning! Did Greeks sometimes make mistakes? So did their gods. They were proud, jealous, lustful, noble, and protective of their favorites. The Greeks made their gods in their own image.

What about the Christian's God? As we'll see, the Christian's God is not so easy to understand. He is a mystery. No one could have "thought up" a God like Him. But on the other hand, when He has shown Himself to us, He is just the way we know deep down that He *should* be.

2 THE MYSTERY OF 3 = 1

Goal: That your students will examine the mystery of God's unity and Trinity.

One of the most mysterious but important truths about God is that He's both three and one at the same time.

Pass out copies of "Our Three-in-One God" (Action Sheet 2A), and work through the first section of the sheet as a class. On the second section, have students work in pairs to show how each of the given references supports the idea of the Trinity. The

questions from the sheet are reprinted for you here along with the Scripture, additional questions, and possible answers your students might give.

I. One God

Israel was surrounded by pagan nations who believed in a lot of gods. These nations were always tempting the people of Israel to follow these gods. What does Moses say in Deuteronomy 6:4, 5 to counteract the temptation to worship many gods?

"Hear, O Israel: The Lord our God, the Lord is one. Love the Lord your God with all your heart and with all your soul and with all your strength" (Deut. 6:4, 5).

Moses says that the Lord our God is *one* Lord—the people must worship Him with all their hearts, souls, and might. There is no room for divided loyalties.

Why does verse 5 naturally follow, if verse 4 is true? Help kids understand that if God is one, we don't have to wonder which God to follow. Our loyalty belongs fully to the one true God. When we know what God is like, we know what He demands of us.

Israel learned by experience that God allows no rivals—either as opponents or as helpers. Even most demons and angels remain nameless; they can't be mistaken for other gods. God demands *all* our love.

How do you think God's oneness separates Him from the "other gods" of this world? Make sure kids see that God's oneness is a quality as well as a quantity. That is, because

He is one, He is reliable. He will not contradict Himself or act against His own desires. The mythical "gods" of this world were always fighting among themselves for the privilege of being "top dog" among many gods. God has no worry from the competition.

How does Isaiah 43:10b, 11 support this view?

"Before me no god was formed, nor will there be one after me. I, even I, am the Lord, and apart from me there is no savior" (Isaiah 43:10b, 11).

(These verses bring the message that the Lord is the one, true God. There was never a true God before Him, and there never will be another true God. The Lord is the only One who brings salvation.)

At this point, have students begin working in pairs.

II. Three-in-One

Suppose you had to describe the idea of the Trinity to a friend at school who had never heard of it before. What would you say?

Explain how each of the following references supports the idea of the Trinity: Hebrews 1:3; John 1:1; 5:23; 14:8, 9, 26; Philippians 2:5, 6, 9, 10; Acts 5:3, 4; Matthew 28:19; II Corinthians 3:17; 13:14.

Possible student answers:

Hebrews 1:3. (This verse declares that Jesus Christ is the exact likeness of God. Christ upholds all things by His powerful Word, and He sits at the right hand of the Majesty on High.)

John 1:1. (The Word, Jesus Christ, is said to be God.)

John 5:23. (In this verse honor for the Son is equated with honor for the Father.)

John 14:8, 9. (Jesus tells Philip that whoever has seen Him has also seen the Father. They are one.)

John 14:26. (The Holy Spirit will be sent by the Father in the name of Christ. The implication is that the Holy Spirit is similar to Christ or equal to Him.)

Philippians 2:5, 6, 9, 10. (Jesus Christ was in the form of God and equal with God. Now God has exalted Him so that everyone in Heaven and earth shall bow at the name of Jesus.)

Acts 5:3, 4. (The Holy Spirit is God; lying against the Holy Spirit is lying to God.)

II Corinthians 3:17. (The Lord and the Spirit are identified with each other.)

II Corinthians 13:14. (All three Persons play an active role in the life of believers, giving grace, love, and fellowship.) Now direct all students to look together at the following text.

Matthew 28:19: "Therefore go and make disciples of all nations, baptizing them in the name of the Father and of the Son and of the Holy Spirit."

What could putting the Father, Son, and Spirit together like this tell us? (That they are all in the same "category," that is, divine.) **Why does**

Jesus not say "names" (plural) rather than "name"? (Maybe to avoid the impression that there are three separate Gods.)

"Name" in Hebrew thought referred to character as well as being a label. Thus all three share the same character—they are God.

Going back to Jesus' baptism (see Luke 3:22), note that the voice, obviously coming from God the Father, speaks to Jesus, God the Son. And in other places the Son speaks to the Father; for example, John 17.

What can we learn from the fact that the Father and Son talk with each other? Remember Jesus' baptism. (It means that they must be "separate" or "individual" enough for conversation between them to be possible. Thus there is not just one God wearing three masks.)

For hundreds of years Christians have tried to find ways to express the mystery of how God is three Persons in one. But it's very difficult. We have trouble imagining how three can equal one. So we use analogies—comparisons—to show how God is like some things we can better understand. Let's look at some good analogies.

Distribute copies of "Like God or Not?" (Action Sheet 2B). Have your kids fill in the chart, explaining how each analogy is like God and how it is different. When kids finish, go over their answers. The analogies and possible answers are given below.

1. A musical chord played on piano or guitar. (A chord is composed of several separate notes, all produced in exactly the same way and at the same time. Played separately, each note is distinguishable in tone from the others; yet together they form a single unified sound. A chord is unlike Persons of the Trinity in that it doesn't have a will, it can't reason, etc.)

2. A basketball team during a game. (Each player has a slightly different job, but all cooperate to score points and win the game. We think of the team as a unit in terms of the game score and league standing. Members communicate with each other during a game. A team is unlike the Trinity in that not all team members are equal in ability, and there may be division and confusion among them.)

3. A car engine. (The engine is composed of a number of different parts, each performing a separate function, but all combining to make the car move. However, these parts do not communicate and are made in some cases of different materials.)

4. The three sides of a triangle. (Each side is necessary in order to form a triangle. But no side is a triangle. Each side is incomplete—without the others, it is only a line. God, on the other hand, isn't incomplete.)

If you have time, let kids explain other analogies they've heard. Give them a chance to think up their own analogies. Wrap up this part of the session by having kids summarize what they have learned about God.

3 TAKING GOD HOME

Goal: That your students will commit themselves to learning about God through His Word.

Suppose as you are leaving today, one of your classmates says to you, "I don't see any point to learning all that stuff about the Trinity and theology. No one has ever seen God anyway, so it's all a bunch of guesses. Besides, it doesn't matter what you believe about God, as long as you're sincere in your beliefs."

How would you respond to what he said? (Allow students to answer. As needed, supplement answers with the following information.)

Our ideas about God are never complete, but we have a true and reliable source from which to draw our conclusions—the Bible. Since Jesus Christ is God, His nature tells us a lot about the way God is. People who worship other gods may really believe what they're doing, but they're still wrong. The Bible still says there's only one way to Heaven, and that's Jesus Christ. Theology is simply careful study of the Bible's truth in order to know more about God.

What are some good ways in which we can get a better "picture" of God? (Some possible answers: reading the Bible, not because we have to, but to let God speak through His Word; daily devotions in which we meditate on God's character and our relationship with Him; communicating with Him in prayer; considering carefully what others have written or said about God in books, Sunday School class, or sermons.)

Encourage students to plan a daily devotional time to further their personal relationships with God. **I want to suggest that we agree to individually spend time each day this week learning more about God through Bible reading and prayer. How long a time do you think we should set for this week?** (Many students will be ready for only about five minutes a day at this point; some will be unwilling to commit to any time at all.) **During this time, try reading a short passage of the Bible and ask yourself what it tells you about God. Record what you discover. Think about what God is like and pray about things that concern you. Think about what God might be saying to you.**

As we close in prayer, let's ask God to help us learn more about Him on our own this week.

GOD, OUR FATHER

Session Aim

That your students will understand what it means to be children of their Heavenly Father through faith in Christ Jesus.

Key Verse

"If you, then, though you are evil, know how to give good gifts to your children, how much more will your Father in heaven give good gifts to those who ask him!" (Matthew 7:11).

Things You'll Need

- *"Our Fatherly God" (Action Sheet 3A)*
- *"If God Were Here . . ." (Action Sheet 3B)*
- *Paper, pencils, tape*
- *Chalkboard and chalk, or newsprint and markers*

"Our Heavenly Father." We've all heard that phrase. But what does it really mean? What is so significant about God being our Father?

To some who have grown up in the church, God as our Father may be a concept simply accepted without much thought. To some who come from single-parent homes or whose earthly fathers don't provide a good example, the idea of "father" may seem vague or negative. Both kinds of kids need healthy concepts of both earthly and heavenly fatherhood. That's why we're looking at the Fatherhood of God in this session.

We'll examine passages of Scripture that help explain various facets of God's Fatherhood. We'll be looking at how our Heavenly Father loves us and cares for us, and at what those things mean in our lives.

Use this lesson to help your kids gain a healthier concept of God the Father, and to guide them into a closer relationship with Him.

1 AN AD FOR A DAD

Goal: That your students will express what they feel are the duties and qualifications of a father.

All of us had no choice about who our fathers would be. But what if the system changed, and you could choose your father as an employer chooses someone for a job? What qualities would you look for in a father? What would you expect of him?

Pass out paper and pencil to each person. It might be helpful to have several pages of "Help Wanted" ads for kids to look at.

To inform applicants about your expectations, make up an advertisement giving the duties of a father and the qualifications he must have. The ad can be in the form of a radio announcement or a "Help Wanted" classified ad in the daily newspaper.

While kids are writing, make a chart titled, "Wanted: Father." Divide a chalkboard or piece of newsprint into three columns. At the top of the first column write "Qualifications." At the top of the second column, write "Duties." Leave the third column blank for now.

After several minutes, have kids read their ads to the class. As kids read, capsulize the qualifications and duties they mention and list them under the appropriate heading on the chart. If possible, write the list in a form which will allow for comparison with God's fatherly characteristics later on. For example, if someone says, "My father must be a millionaire," you could write, "Material wealth."

A few of the things mentioned could be contrary to the traits of a good father, but list them anyway. Leave the chart up; you'll use it again later.

2 OUR FATHERLY GOD

Goal: That your students will identify some of God's fatherly characteristics and will describe His relationship with His special children.

Today's Bible study shows how God acts as a father. Distribute copies of "Our Fatherly God" (Action Sheet 3A), and have kids answer the first two questions individually or in small groups. When most of your kids are ready, go over their answers.

For your convenience, the questions and possible answers are printed for you here.

1. We sometimes refer to God the Father as the Creator. List three creative things He did according to Acts 17:24-28. Be specific.

Here is the passage: "The God who made the world and everything in it is the Lord of heaven and earth and does not live in temples built by hands. And he is not served by human hands, as if he needed anything, because he himself gives all men life and breath and everything else. From one man he made every nation of men, that they should inhabit the whole earth; and he determined the times set for them and the exact places where they should live. God did this so that men would seek him and perhaps reach out for him and find him, though he is not far from each one of us. 'For in him we live and move and have our being.' As some of your own poets have said, 'We are his offspring.' "

(Don't let kids get away with general answers like "He created the world." Probe for more specific answers: He gives life and breath to everything; He established the ongoing human race; He gave people freedom and set limits; He set up potential for contact with people.)

2. God created people, and in doing that He became the Father of everyone—Christians and non-Christians. But He is uniquely the Father of those who are living examples of Galatians 3:26. How would you explain that verse to someone who says to you, "God is everyone's Father. What's so special about Christians?"

Here is the verse: "You are all sons of God through faith in Christ Jesus."

(Answers will vary, depending on your kids' Bible knowledge. Any answer that indicates faith in Jesus Christ is correct. Examples: Christians are new people; Christians have the Holy Spirit living in them; Christians are adopted into God's family; Christians have access to God in prayer, have their sins forgiven in Christ, have eternal life.)

Work together on question 3, having kids call out answers as someone writes them down on a chalkboard or newsprint.

3. Read Matthew 6:6-13; then fill out the chart below, using all of the Scriptures we've looked at so far in this session.

Here is the Matthew passage: "When you pray, go into your room, close the door and pray to your Father, who is unseen. Then your Father, who sees what is done in secret, will reward you. And when you pray, do not keep on babbling like pagans, for they think they will be heard because of their many words. Do not be like them, for your Father knows what you need before you ask him.

"This, then, is how you should pray:

" 'Our Father in heaven, hallowed be your name, your kingdom come, your will be done on earth as it is in heaven. Give us today our daily bread. Forgive us our debts, as we also have forgiven our debtors. And lead us not into temptation, but deliver us from the evil one.' "

Students' answers should include the following ideas:

What God Does for Us
(Gives human life
Rewards us for faithful prayer
Gives food and forgiveness
Limits the difficulty of our testing
Protects us from Satan
Forgives our sins)

What God Asks of Us
(Communication through prayer
Humility
Praise and honor
Living in the hope of what is to come
Understanding of what Christ did for us)

As our Heavenly Father, God has done great things for us. Our small actions of obedience can't come close to repaying Him for what He has done. Obeying Him should be part of our thankfulness for His reaching down to save us through Christ.

4. Read Matthew 7:11. How is God the Father similar to a good earthly father? How is He different? Summarize your answers to these two questions in two or three sentences.

Here is the verse: "If you, then, though you are evil, know how to give good gifts to your children, how much more will your Father in heaven give good gifts to those who ask him!"

(Encourage kids to think about what Matthew 7:11 implies. Suggest that no one write anything in the first minute; ask kids to think before writing. Then discuss their answers.)

3 LIFE WITH THE FATHER

Goal: That your students will identify the most appropriate responses to God the Father, and begin to make those responses.

Now have your kids look back at the characteristics of a good earthly father which they listed earlier. At the top of the third column, write "God's Characteristics." Looking at the other columns, have kids suggest traits that might be the same and ones that might be different. When you've completed the chart, discuss the following question.

If you had such a father, how would you react to him? If you knew he was in the room with you, how would your actions and feelings be affected?

(Answers may vary; some students will mention negative feelings, and others will be more positive. Once the flow of answers stops, emphasize that the feelings and actions they mentioned are responses to who that father is. They would react differently to a father with different characteristics.)

The way we respond to God the Father also depends on who we know He is. Let's look at what happens when we really are aware that God is present.

Before class, cut apart the cards on "If God Were Here" (Action Sheet 3B). Now pin or tape one of the cards to the back of each of your kids, without letting kids see what is on their own cards. If you have more than ten kids, make extra copies of the cards. Explain that the cards contain responses we might have if we realized that God the Father was physically present with us in the room. Have kids ask each other only questions which can be answered with a yes or a no, seeking to discover what the responses are that are pinned on their backs. Let kids wander around while they work on this. Some of these might be tough, so give kids some hints if they start getting discouraged.

Here are the responses that are on the cards:

- Bow down and worship
- Seek to live holy lives
- Try to love others more fully
- Get excited about serving God
- Develop a desire to learn from Him
- Gain confidence against Satan
- Feel the peace of God's love
- Feel the guilt of unconfessed sin
- Desire to remain with Him
- Realize how small we are

As kids get started, erase the characteristics of an earthly father from the chalkboard, or turn over a new sheet if you're using newsprint. List the responses from the cards as kids discover what those responses are. Have kids compare those responses with God's characteristics, and draw connections wherever possible. They might want to add to the characteristics list at this time.

Only those who personally know God as their Father can really respond in the ways we listed. How would you respond to God right now?

(Allow volunteers to give their responses. Don't apply pressure for kids to answer.)

There may be kids in your class who have not trusted Christ as their Savior. This would be a good time to present God's offer of salvation. Remember, however, to tailor your presentation to the characteristics of your class. For instance, in a small group, one non-Christian might be afraid to respond to a public appeal. In any case, let students know you want to talk to them privately if they have any uncertainty in this area. Writing your home phone number on the board may help convince students of your willingness to spend time with them out of class.

Encourage kids to remember the responses you listed—and to remember that God really *is* present all the time. Ask kids to especially concentrate on that awareness this week, and to be ready to tell you what happened when you meet again.

Have several kids close in prayer, asking that God will make them aware of His presence throughout the week.

COMPLETE IN CHRIST

Session Aim

That your students will grow in their conviction that Christ is God's Son, worthy of highest loyalty and love.

Key Verse

"For in Christ all the fullness of the Deity lives in bodily form, and you have been given fullness in Christ, who is the head over every power and authority" (Colossians 2:9, 10).

Things You'll Need

- *"Picture the Son" (Action Sheet 4A)*
- *"Jesus, the One and Only" (Action Sheet 4B)*
- *Chalkboard and chalk*
- *Markers and newsprint*

Who can kids trust these days? *Not many of their friends; possibly not brothers or sisters; maybe not their school system; certainly not TV or movies. Usually they can trust their parents—though parents are the last people many kids want to trust.*

Where does that leave today's teenagers? Needing someone they can really trust.

God's Son, Jesus, is the One kids need. He loves them; He intercedes for them; He knows what they're going through. He watches over them; He draws them to Himself; He died for them. As the second Person of the Trinity, He is all God, all Man—uniquely qualified as both Savior and Example.

We sometimes tend to forget just what Christ did and does for us. This session will help your kids learn more about the One who loves them, and will challenge them to praise Him and commit themselves to Him fully.

1

THE PERFECT PARTNER

Goal: That your students will describe the type of person who is worthy of all their loyalty and trust.

Let's say you've decided to start a business of your own. But you need a partner—someone to work with you in your business. This person would have access to all your life's savings and all of your business earnings. Write a description of the kind of person you'd be willing to trust that much. Make a list of qualities you'd want that person to have.

Kids should confine their answers to such things as character traits, attitudes, feelings, life-style, habits, abilities, and actions.

After students finish their lists, have a volunteer read his or her list aloud while you write the items on a chalkboard or newsprint. Using this list as a starting point, ask others to contribute items that haven't yet been mentioned.

Pass out small pieces of paper and have each student write down his or her top three choices. When all the ballots are counted, circle the top three vote getters.

How would you find such a person?

(Such a person would be extremely difficult to find. Few people, if any, measure up to our standards of perfection.)

How could you be sure you'd found such a person?

(At the very least, it would take years of experience—getting to know the person in many different situations and circumstances. But you may never be sure: some imperfections may not show up for years.)

So it looks like we'd be taking a chance if we committed ourselves totally to another person. Yet there is a Person who asks us to give our lives completely to Him—Jesus Christ. Today we'll find out why we can trust Him completely with our lives.

Divide the class into groups of three or four. Explain that before we can give our lives to someone, we must find out what that person is like. Have each group brainstorm as many answers as possible on this question:

What is so special about Jesus? What makes Christ so different from other people in history?

After three minutes, have each group read its list of characteristics. Write

each on the chalkboard or flip chart. Then move on to the next section of this session.

PICTURE THIS

Goal: That your students will demonstrate their knowledge of Christ by drawing symbolic descriptions of Him.

We already know a lot of facts about Christ. And the Bible gives us a lot of detail about His life. Let's look at two sections that tell us quite a bit about Him.

Distribute copies of "Picture the Son" (Action Sheet 4A) and divide your class into three groups. Assign one of the first three sections of this study to each group. Kids will do the fourth section individually.

Before kids begin working, read the following paragraphs aloud.

Picture this scene: A group of men and women are sitting around talking. After some discussion, one of the men stands up and says, "I am God." When Jesus said something to that effect, the religious leaders in the crowd tried to stone Him. They must have been shocked to hear a man say that.

Shock is only one of several honest ways to respond to Jesus' claim that He is the Son of God. Another way to react is to say, "He doesn't really mean it," or "He means something else." Another response is to laugh

at Him and call the whole idea cra-zy. **Still another reaction is to bow down and worship Him.**

Let's look at some New Testament verses that describe Christ; when we're finished, we'll have to decide what our own response will be.

Supply each group with marking pens and newsprint. If you have enough chalkboard space, you could assign a section of the board to each group instead. Instruct each group to discuss the assignment and share ideas for drawings. Kids may want to practice on scrap paper first.

Tell kids how much time they have for the assignment. When time is up, have each group present its drawing to the class, explaining how that drawing answers the question.

The questions and possible answers are printed for you below. But the an-swers should not be used to impose too many limits on students' work. When dealing with symbolic art like this, you can't really call one answer right and another wrong; the an-swers reflect students' perceptions and impressions. Still, these suggest-ed answers might be useful to you if some students aren't quite sure what is called for or if they have trouble getting started. If either situation arises, you could use elements of these answers as examples.

1. Use words, lines, or symbols to describe God the Son as He is pic-tured in Hebrews 1:2, 3.

(Christ might be depicted as a speak-er, a messenger, an heir or owner of all things, a creator, a radiant or powerful being, a representative, a purifier, or as seated at the Father's right hand.)

Which of the descriptive phrases in Hebrews 1:3 means the most to you right now? Why?

(If the group has not provided a uni-fied answer to this question, ask for volunteers from the group to answer it individually.)

2. Use lines, words, symbols to show the relationship between God the Father, God the Son, and the angels. Hebrews 1:4-8, and John 1:1-3. (The angel part is easy, but double-check the relationship be-tween Father and Son.)

(Students' drawings should imply that the Father and Son are interre-lated, that neither is inferior to the other, and that both are superior to the angels. These ideas can be de-picted in many ways.)

3. Read John 1:4-10. The Word is Jesus. With words, symbols, and stick figures, explain what is hap-pening in these verses. To do this, you will have to identify what is meant by light and darkness.

(Drawings might show Jesus with the Father, active in creating the uni-verse, radiating light, or living among people and perhaps being rejected by them. "Light" and "darkness" could refer to truth and falsehood, good and evil, the power of God and the power of the Devil, or life and death.)

After all three groups have given their presentations, ask students to study the drawings for a moment and to mentally review what they have learned about Christ. Then have them individually write their answers to question 4. After a few minutes, ask several students to read their answers aloud.

4. Someone says Jesus was just a good man, a great teacher. Respond by completing the sentences:

A. Wrong, according to (insert verse from today's text) _______, Jesus is
_______.

B. Wrong, according to (insert verse from today's text) _______, Jesus is
_______.

C. Wrong, according to (insert verse from today's text) _______, Jesus is
_______.

Here are some possible answers:

Hebrews 1:2—God's Son; Heir of all things; Creator.

Hebrews 1:3—has God's glory; is the exact image of God; sustains all things; washed away our sins; is equal with God.

Hebrews 1:4—superior to angels; has a more excellent name than angels do.

Hebrews 1:5—Son of God.

Hebrews 1:6—worshiped by all the angels.

Hebrews 1:8—has an eternal Kingdom and a scepter of righteousness; is God.

John 1:1—is eternal; is God.

John 1:2—eternal.

3 THE INCREDIBLE SON

Goal: That your students will examine the uniqueness of Jesus as God's Son and respond to Him in praise and commitment.

Pass out copies of "Jesus, the One and Only" (Action Sheet 4B) to your kids. Give them a few minutes to read over their sheets, and then discuss them one section at a time along the following lines.

HIS INCREDIBLE AUTHORITY

Why do you think the New Testament tells us so much about Christ's authority? How do you think we should feel about His authority?

(Because Jesus lived as a servant, we might not know about His authority if the Bible didn't tell us; when we know about Christ's authority, we can respond. Our response to His authority should be trust, obedience, respect, and confidence.)

HIS ASTONISHING WISDOM

If Jesus were to appear on a television talk show, how do you think

the audience would react to His wisdom? How do you think He might display His wisdom?

(They might be hostile and make fun of Him, as people did the first time He came to earth. He might display His wisdom as He did the first time—by showing people He knew the real motives for their actions.)

HIS SERVANT ATTITUDE

What things might keep us from serving others the way Jesus did?

(Pride, embarrassment, opinion of others, lack of love for the other person, self-centered attitude, prejudice, fear of failure.)

HIS PERFECT LOVE

Name some ways in which Jesus showed His unselfish love for those He met. How can we show that kind of love for people we meet?

(He healed sickness, raised people from the dead, comforted sad people, prayed for people, went out of His way to help, suffered and died for others. We may not be able to do all of those things, but we can do some of them.)

HIS POWERFUL RESURRECTION

Why is the Resurrection so important to Christians?

(It proves Christ is God, shows Christ is alive, shows He is powerful enough to help us, gives us assurance of our own resurrection.)

HIS FUTURE RETURN

How can we show by our lives that we expect Christ to return soon?

(Urgency in telling others about Him, faithful service, holy lives.)

After going over "Jesus, the One and Only," challenge your kids to respond to Christ. Ask for two responses:

Praise

Have kids think of one or two key points about Christ which they have learned today. Then encourage kids to pray sentence prayers in which they tell God what that new knowledge about Christ means to them. For instance, if one student learned more about Jesus' love today, she might pray, "Jesus, Your love for me makes me want to share Your love with others." Continue this praise session until all who wish to have had a chance to pray.

Commitment

Give your kids an opportunity to commit their lives to Christ. Some may never have asked Christ to be their Savior; briefly tell students how they may accept Him. Some of your kids may have been taking their Christianity for granted and may need to reaffirm their relationships with Christ.

After a few moments of silence, encourage kids who have made commitments to Christ to remain after the session is over or to contact you during the coming week. Close the session in prayer, thanking God for what He has done in the lives of your kids. Be sure to talk and pray with any kids who remain. Arrange a follow-up meeting with each one for the coming week.

THE COMFORTER AND ME

Session Aim

That your students will know that life in Christ gives a person unlimited resources through the Holy Spirit.

Key Verses

"And I will ask the Father, and he will give you another Counselor to be with you forever—the Spirit of truth. The world cannot accept him, because it neither sees him nor knows him. But you know him, for he lives with you and will be in you" (John 14:16, 17).

Things You'll Need

- *"The Parable of the Wireless Wonder" (Action Sheet 5A)*
- *"Spirit Search Group Assignments" (Action Sheet 5B)*
- *Bibles*
- *Paper, pencils*
- *Your pastor or other church leader to discuss your church's teaching on the Holy Spirit (optional)*

Your kids may already feel they know a lot about God, and probably about Jesus, too. But it's not too likely that they are confident about their knowledge of the Holy Spirit. The Holy Spirit seems to be seen as the "silent partner" of the Godhead by many people. But He really does have an active ministry in our Christian lives—a ministry that we couldn't last long without.

This session will help your kids see who the Holy Spirit really is and why He was sent to us. They'll examine how He worked in Bible times and how He works today. They'll also be challenged to seek more of the Holy Spirit's working in their own lives.

1 AN INNER BUZZ?

Goal: That your students will begin thinking about some of the functions of the Holy Spirit.

Suppose someone could invent a machine that would warn you every time you thought about doing something you knew was wrong. Let's see what might happen by reading "The Parable of the Wireless Wonder" (Action sheet 5A).

Give all your kids copies of this parable, and read it aloud as kids follow along. Then discuss:

As we saw in the parable, the Holy Spirit often acts like an "inner buzzer." But He is also much more. What else can the Holy Spirit do in a Christian's life?

(He is a conscience, a comforter, a source of power, and a guide.)

We need the Holy Spirit. The more we know about Him, the more we can use His unlimited power. Unfortunately, many people, even Christians, don't know much about the Holy Spirit. Let's see some of what the Bible says about the Holy Spirit's work.

2 SPIRIT SEARCH

Goal: That your students will examine several passages of Scripture to expand their knowledge of the Holy Spirit.

First, let's find out how much we do know about the Holy Spirit.

Divide your class into two teams. Instruct each team to come up with a list of things they know about the Holy Spirit, without using their Bibles. Set a time limit (three or four minutes might be enough), and have the teams race to see who can think of the highest number of different things about the Holy Spirit.

Have your teams report, and give credit for any answer that is pretty close to being right. Your kids will probably have trouble coming up with many responses. They might include: given by the Father; will be with them forever; cannot be seen; is present with us; guides and helps us.

Discuss your kids' answers briefly, and compliment both teams for their efforts.

You've come up with good answers. But there is a lot more we can learn about the Holy Spirit. Let's look at John 14:15-21 and see what we find there.

Have kids read John 14:15-21 and look at the "Spirit Search" section of Action Sheet 5A. Read the introduction on the sheet; then go over the questions together, one at a time. The questions and possible answers are printed for you here.

1. In verse 16, what name did Jesus give the Holy Spirit? How does the name describe His function?

Let your kids give their ideas, then give them some of the following information:

The Greek word translated "Comforter" might better be translated "Helper." The word might literally be translated "one called alongside." The idea is that of one being there to help when needed.

2. What does it mean to us that Jesus promised "one called alongside"?

(Jesus wanted to be sure we have the support we need—someone to help us.)

3. Jesus commanded something before He promised the Holy Spirit. What was that command?

(The command was that if they loved Christ, they were to keep His commandments [vs. 15]. Since Christ was going away, the disciples would need outside help.)

4. Why do you think Christ referred to the Comforter as the Spirit of Truth?

(The Spirit helps Christians understand the truths of their beliefs. These truths struggle to exist in a world filled with contrary opinions and error. The Spirit also helps Christians organize their lives around a new and true center—Christ.)

5. What does the word "comfortless" (vs. 18) mean?

(Students will probably say something like, "without help" or "unhappy and alone.")

The word can be translated "orphans." It indicates a sense of shock, sadness, and loss that an orphan feels.

6. What event was Jesus talking about when He used the phrase "little while" (vs. 19)?

(The Crucifixion. People saw Jesus until that time. Between the time He arose from the dead and ascended, only His followers saw Him. Following His ascension, the disciples knew His presence as the Holy Spirit lived in them.)

7. Verse 19 indicates that believers will see Jesus. Since He is in Heaven, how does Jesus show Himself to His followers today?

(Through the Holy Spirit, the promised Comforter, who lives in them. Just as the Spirit was given to the disciples to help them obey Christ's commandments, so He is given to all believers to enable them to meet the problems of life in a Christ-pleasing way.)

Now divide your kids into three investigative teams, and give each team one of the "Spirit Search Group Assignments" from Action Sheet 5B. Let the teams work on their assignment sheets for about ten minutes; then bring them back together to report.

The Team Assignments are printed for you here, along with possible responses:

We're expanding our Spirit search! Each investigative team has an assignment to complete. Once all our assignments have been completed, we can put together a report on who the Holy Spirit really is.

Team X Assignment

Here are your questions. Use the Scriptures below (or any other ones you can find) and search out the most accurate and complete answers you can.

Where does the Holy Spirit come from? What part does He play in the Christian's life? What are some of the things He does? Make a list of as many things as you can find.

Scriptures to check: John 14:15-21; 15:26; 20:21, 22; Hebrews 9:14; Romans 8:9, 14-16; Galatians 5:22, 23; I Corinthians 6:19; 12:7, 11; Titus 3:5.

(The Holy Spirit is eternal. He was sent into our world by God the Father. He enters the life of each person who invites Him in. He is constantly at work, helping to develop love, joy, peace, patience, kindness, gentleness, righteousness, etc.)

Team Y Assignment

Here are your questions. Use the Scriptures below (or any other ones you can find) and search out the most accurate and complete answers you can. What was the difference in the function of the Holy Spirit in the Old Testament and the New Testament? List some of the special things He did in the Old Testament.

Scriptures to check: John 7:39; Genesis 1:2; Job 33:4; Judges 3:10; 14:6; Exodus 31:3; I Samuel 16:13; Nehemiah 9:20.

(The Holy Spirit did not live within every believer in the Old Testament. He only came upon people on special occasions when God knew they needed special guidance and power. He was *with* them, not *in* them. The Holy Spirit helped different people gain strength, develop skills, and become effective leaders. He was also involved in an unusual project—the creation of the world!)

Team Z Assignment

Here are your questions. Use the Scriptures below (or any other ones you can find) and search out the most accurate and complete answers you can. What can you find out about the personality of the Holy Spirit? What is He like? List as many qualities as you can.

Scriptures to check: I Corinthians 2:11, 12; 12:11; Romans 8:4, 14, 16, 26, 27; 15:30; Galatians 4:6; Ephesians 4:30; Psalm 139:7-10; Isaiah 11:2; John 14:15-21; 20:21, 22.

(The Holy Spirit is righteous, concerned, loving, and always present. He wills [makes decisions], grieves, and pleads for believers. He is full of knowledge and wisdom.)

Now have each team summarize its report in ten words or less. Combine the three reports into a summary report on the Holy Spirit. After completing your summary, move on to the next section of this session.

3 PLUGGED IN

Goal: That your students will seek the Holy Spirit's working in their lives.

We've talked about who the Holy Spirit is, what He's like, what He does, and what He can do in a Christian's life.

Now, how can a person have the Holy Spirit in his or her life, and start using the Holy Spirit's tremendous power?

NOTE: This would be a good time to explain what your church teaches about the power and working of the Holy Spirit in the world today. If possible, have your pastor come in to talk and answer questions.

Most Christians agree that four prerequisites to being filled and controlled by the Holy Spirit are:

• Being cleansed from all known sin (I John 1:7-9; II Cor. 7:1);

• Giving full control of one's life to God without any reservation (Romans 12:1; 6:13);

• Believing that God will fill with the Holy Spirit all those who confess their sins and surrender themselves to Him (Romans 4:20, 21);

• Accepting by faith that one has already been filled by the Spirit, and acting upon that belief.

Those of us who have asked Jesus to be our Savior have the Holy Spirit's power available to us. God the Holy Spirit lives in us. God helps us. Perhaps you've never thought about ways in which the Holy Spirit has helped you. Today we're going to do this.

Read the following statements to your kids one at a time, and have kids volunteer to respond. You may have to respond first to get kids started. Don't let a few moments of silence frighten you. Let kids think for a while and wait for their responses. Try to get all of your kids to respond to at least one, if not all, of the statements.

Think of a time when:

• **The Holy Spirit helped you witness for Christ.**

• **You were thinking about doing something wrong and something made you remember how Christ would feel about your action.**

• **You were worried about something and the Holy Spirit guided you to Scripture or to someone who could help you.**

• **You hesitated to do something good, but then you felt something prodding you to go ahead and do it.**

We've just seen how the Holy Spirit has worked in our lives. And there are certainly more ways that we can't think of or aren't even aware of. The fact that we have the Holy Spirit with us always is a reason for great rejoicing.

As you wrap up today's session, have your kids write prayers of thanks to God for His gift of the Holy Spirit. First, go over the four prerequisites to being filled and controlled by the Holy Spirit, which were mentioned earlier. Encourage your kids to examine their lives and to ask that the Holy Spirit help them in areas where they are having problems.

Also encourage kids to thank God in their prayers for specific times the Holy Spirit has helped them. If you have time, you might let your kids write their prayers in the form of songs, to be sung to a familiar tune. Let volunteers read their prayers or sing their songs.

THE CREATOR OF ALL

Session Aim

That your students will see God as the Creator of all things.

Key Verse

"You are worthy, our Lord and God, to receive glory and honor and power, for you created all things, and by your will they were created and have their being" (Revelation 4:11).

Things You'll Need

● *"A Conversation Overheard" (Action Sheet 6A)*
● *"What's So Special About People?" (Action Sheet 6B)*
● *Two good readers for Action Sheet 6A*
● *Bibles, pencils*

The origins of the universe and its inhabitants are at the center of controversy today. Is "creationism" simply a religious belief that has no basis in fact? Is evolution the only acceptable explanation for the origin of life? Can an intelligent, educated person still believe that God made the earth? Kids and adults face these questions when standing up for belief in a Creator God.

This session will help your kids see that we can be confident in our belief that God created us and the world around us. And your students will be motivated to thank God for His creative work in their lives.

1 BY FAITH OR BY FAITH?

Goal: That your students will see that those who believe in creation by evolution as well as those who believe in creation by God have to accept some parts of their belief by faith.

Distribute copies of "A Conversation Overheard" (Action Sheet 6A). As the class follows along, have two good readers present the conversation, taking the two roles in the article.

If your students have trouble reading without preparation, consider giving two students their copies of "A Conversation Overheard" ahead of time so that they can practice it. Present this mini-lecture after the kids read the article:

Christians sometimes argue about the exact way in which God created people and the world, but no Christian should have any trouble answering the question, "Where did it all come from?" It all came from God. Christians have a basic belief in God. All their other beliefs come from their faith that there is an all-powerful God.

People who don't know God can give lots of answers, but eventually they get to the point where they don't know where it all came from. They have to make guesses or assumptions, and go ahead having faith that their guesses are right.

Neither the Christian nor the atheist can prove in courtroom style with visible evidence that he or she is right and the other person is wrong. Each accepts his or her view on faith.

The Christian has faith that God exists. The atheist believes God does not exist and this takes faith, too. Both the Christian and the atheist have faith. This is an important fact to remember if someone tries to make you feel foolish and uneducated for believing in a Creator God.

It may seem to you that much more time is spent, perhaps in school and

with non-Christian friends, talking about creation of people without God than creation by God. So let's spend some time now talking about the Christian's faith in what the Bible says about God and the creation of human beings.

2 IN WHOSE IMAGE?

Goal: That your students will become familiar with the Christian's belief that God created the world, and that He created people in His own image.

Have your kids read Genesis 1:1-5, 24-26. Then have kids respond to the following question.

If you were to summarize this passage in one sentence, what would you say?

Let several kids make suggestions.

Before we go any further, let's get a couple of very important facts in focus:

The Bible is not a textbook on science—it is the story of salvation. So we can't expect it to answer all scientific questions.

The emphasis of the story of creation is on the Creator—not the creation. God doesn't emphasize how He created. Instead He makes it clear who created: He did!

Pass out copies of "What's So Special About People?" (Action sheet 6B). Go over it with your kids, reading the informative parts, and discussing each question. The questions have been reprinted for you here, along with possible answers.

What's So Special About People?

Push your mind back in time to the very beginning—to the awesome time when "In the beginning God created the heavens and the earth" (Genesis 1:1). God created a universe so huge we can't find the end of it, suns, moons, plants, animals, and finally humans. God said, "Let us make man in our image, in our likeness. . . . So God created man in his own image . . . male and female he created them" (Genesis 1:26, 27).

1. Look up Acts 17:26. What does this section from one of Paul's sermons tell you about creation?

(God created humans with a plan in mind. He wanted people to seek after Him.)

Humans are special in God's creation. He "formed" man and woman instead of just calling them into existence like everything else in creation. And He formed us *in His image!*

Only people can reason. Only people have a conscience—a sense of right and wrong. This means we have the tremendous opportunity of knowing and loving God!

Sure, our bodies resemble those of certain animals. We all had the same Designer! But our spirits, our souls,

God made like Himself—to be able to do what is right, to reason, to be creative, to love Him, to be responsible to Him.

You're made in God's image: you're special!

2. Why do you think the Bible doesn't tell us everything about creation, especially since so many people have such trouble believing it?

(The Bible isn't trying to give all the scientific answers. By not telling us everything, it causes us to exercise faith in God. What the Bible does indicate about the Creation is that it was orderly, deliberately planned, and completed with the creation of man.)

One problem in accepting the Biblical account as accurate is the apparent vast age of the earth. The Bible doesn't seem to allow for so much passage of time. There are five basic theories that try to match the apparent age of the earth with the Genesis account. You might want to share this information with your kids now:

1. Some say that the Genesis account is a poetic or pictorial arrangement of the fact that God created all things in an orderly manner. God did not use the language of science since it changes; so He chose the universal language of poetry to express truths about His creation—and that He is the Creator.

2. Another theory suggests that these were days of revelation rather than creation. In other words, God told the story of creation to Moses over a seven-day period, and he then wrote Genesis. The days would refer to what God revealed to Moses each time.

3. Another theory suggests that the first two verses of Genesis refer to the creation of the basis for matter (energy) and the development of the vast universe. For example, the galaxy to which earth belongs has over 30 billion suns—and at least 100,000 such galaxies exist. Genesis 1:3, according to this theory, begins a general account of the creation of the earth, culminating with mankind's creation.

4. A fourth theory supposes a dateless gap between Genesis 1:1 and 1:2. Those who hold this theory believe the earth was once inhabited by beings who rebelled against the Creator and thus caused the earth to fall into chaos. According to this theory, the geological ages occurred during this "gap." The theory is sometimes called "Pember's Theory" and was once widely popularized. No real evidence exists for this theory.

5. Another theory is that the "days" of creation were not 24-hour periods, but indefinite periods of time. The Hebrew word for day (*yom*—with a long "o") is used elsewhere in the Bible to refer to periods of time other than the 24-hour day (see Psalms 20:1; 90:4).

Obviously the complete case for each theory cannot be presented here. The Christian will want to study further before committing himself to a position. Remember, however, that the emphasis must be on the Creator. Christians can disagree over the details of creation without affecting their strong faith in the truth that God *is* the Creator.

3. Since all people are made in the image of God, how do you think you should feel about yourself?

(Answers might be along these lines: Since God used Himself as a model in making me, I should respect myself more; I have a purpose that is as special as I am; I am worthwhile to God, so what does it matter if some other kids say I'm no good?)

4. How should you think about others?

(Students should realize that since all people are created in God's image, each person is of equal importance to Him. Each person deserves respect from other people.)

5. If we believe that people are unique, the highest level of God's creation, what difference does it make?

(Because God created us that way, He is concerned about us. We can't afford to ignore God, because He made us able to communicate and respond to Him.)

6. What might an evolutionist say is the purpose of man?

(There is no spiritual purpose for man, because there is no spiritual Creator. If man evolved without an orderly plan of Creation, there can be no plan of life goals beyond the physical and material.)

7. What does the Creation story tell us about the purpose of man?

(People are to take care of the rest of God's creation. Because people are made in God's image, they have a responsibility to God. God made the Creation to bring glory to Himself, so people are to bring glory to God also. People have a spiritual purpose.)

The Key Verse for this lesson summarizes our discussion of God and His created world:

Revelation 4:11: "You are worthy, our Lord and God, to receive glory and honor and power, for you created all things, and by your will they were created and have their being."

3 THANKS, GOD!

Goal: That your students will thank God for His creation and for creating people in His image.

So God is the Creator, and man is the highest of His life forms on earth. What does that have to do with the things we do and think every day?

Assign each of the following problem situations to your kids. You might want to number off by fives, giving each student just one situation.

Then have kids report their responses to the entire class.

1. Jim says that since Communists deny God's existence, they don't deserve God's love or ours. What do you say?

2. Heather asks if it is possible to believe in evolution and believe in God.

3. Glen asks how kids today can believe in an old-fashioned idea like the Creation story in Genesis.

4. Your teacher who doesn't believe in God asks students to volunteer ideas about how people were created and to explain their ideas thoroughly.

5. Lynn wants to know why—if God created people as a perfect creation—they have so much trouble getting along with each other.

As kids report, you might want to guide them a bit by gently questioning weaknesses in their views. Help kids to be ready to respond appropriately in similar situations they might face.

God created us—made us so we can communicate with Him. That's exciting! Let's spend some time today thanking Him for creating people. Think of a very special person you're thankful God created. This could be a friend, parent, anyone. Then thank God for that person and, in your prayer, specifically mention one reason you are thankful for that person.

When kids have finished, ask them to think of one person they haven't treated as if that person is a special, important creation of God. Suggest they pray silently, asking God to help them treat everyone with respect, as God wants them to treat someone He made.

I CAN'T? HE CAN!

Session Aim

That your students will learn about and appropriate some of the power of God.

Key Verses

"Now to him who is able to do immeasurably more than all we ask or imagine, according to his power that is at work within us, to him be glory in the church and in Christ Jesus throughout all generations, for ever and ever! Amen" (Ephesians 3:20, 21).

Things You'll Need

- *"God Power" (Action Sheet 7A)*
- *Mini-poster (Action Sheet 7B)*
- *Bibles*
- *Paper, pencils*

How can kids live successful Christian lives in an anti-Christian world? They can't—not without the supernatural power God offers them.

As Christians, we worship the all-powerful Creator of the Universe—a Creator who loves us and empowers us. He can give kids the help they need to make it through the troubles they face.

Use this session to help your kids see the extent of God's power and to encourage them to draw on that power.

1 TO BE OR NOT TO BE?

Goal: That your students will conduct a mathematical experiment to demonstrate how nearly impossible it would be for human life to form by chance.

God knows about everything. He knows as much about microbiology and space travel as He does about loaves and fishes. He had it all planned before He made the world.

Yet some people maintain that the world, and everything in it, came about by chance in a slow, gradual way.

Pass out paper and pencils.

We are going to figure out the odds of simple life forming by chance.

Scientists tell us that DNA (deoxyribonucleic acid) is the building block of life. One molecule is only one ten-millionth of an inch long, but it controls heredity and directs production of protein in all living cells.

DNA plus protein equals chromosomes. And chromosomes determine much of our looks, our personality, and certainly decide what species of life we will be.

Therefore, for life to form, as we know it, 24 molecules must arrange themselves in the proper order.

What are the odds of this happening by chance? Figure it out this way: Let's say you have the first two molecules, numbered 1 and 2. The odds of picking out these two molecules in the proper order is 1 x 2 for a probability of one chance in two.

What about three molecules? 1 x 2 x 3 = 6, or 1 chance in six. Using this formula, figure out the odds of getting ten of these molecules in the right order.

(1 x 2 x 3 x 4 x 5 x 6 x 7 x 8 x 9 x 10 = 3,628,800.)

And that's only 10 molecules. For DNA to form, 24 molecules have to come together in the right order!

2 POWER TO SPARE

Goal: That your students will examine how the laws of science demonstrate God's power.

With such overwhelming odds against even one cell of human life "just happening," it seems that more "faith" is required to believe it was the result of chance, than to trust that an all-wise Creator planned and made life.

And if one tiny cell is that complex, how much more are all the stars, planets, galaxies, and constellations?

Have your kids read Genesis 1:14-18; then discuss the following questions:

What does the Bible explain about creation which is left out of scientific explanations?

(It provides the original source of life—God. God was the one who made the visible out of the invisible.)

What does this passage tell us about God's power?

(He is the source of power. He is all-powerful.)

Distribute copies of "God Power" (Action Sheet 7A), and be sure everyone has a Bible and a pencil or pen. Have kids work in pairs for this part of your session. Discuss the questions one at a time when the pairs are finished. The questions and suggested answers are printed for you.

1. You and your friend have just seen a film on the marvels of science. Your friend turns to you and says, "The laws of science seem to point to the fact that the world can run itself without God. Therefore, God must not exist." How would you respond? Read the two passages below and come up with a response based on each.

Job 38:1-11

(First, students might point out that even though creation seems to "run itself," it may not do so indefinitely; stars burn out, the orbits of planets deteriorate, animals die. Even if creation does run itself, that doesn't mean there is no God; it makes sense to believe that someone set it all in motion. In the passage from Job, God asks Job several questions. In His questioning it is understood that God alone was responsible for creating the world [vs. 4]. In fact, God specifically tells Job that He suspended earth in its place in space [vs. 6], and He made the boundaries for the great seas on the earth [vs. 10]. How God did these things no human knows. But if God created all the things of the universe, doesn't it stand to reason that He also designed and works through the scientific principles by which they would work together in harmony?)

Genesis 1:14-18

(In the Genesis passage God states reasons for creating lights to appear in the sky—to separate day and night, to show the time when days, years, and religious festivals begin, to give light to the earth. As we observe the behavior of the sun, moon, and stars from day to day and year to year, we are witnesses of the unfailing scientific principles put into action by our powerful God.)

2. According to the laws that God set up, the sun, moon, and stars all have a specific purpose. What is their purpose according to the Genesis passage you just read? Look also at Psalm 104:19-24.

(The sun, moon, and stars were made to mark time, to give us time to rest, and to cause the seasons for variety and enjoyment.)

3. In writing to the Colossians about Jesus Christ, the apostle Paul talks about an even bigger purpose for all the things of nature. Explain what this purpose is by putting Colossians 1:16, 17 into your own words.

(Paraphrases will vary, but here is one possibility: God created the things in Heaven and earth for Jesus Christ. Christ existed before all these things, and now He actually holds the world together. Only in relation to Him does anything have meaning.)

4. These verses tell us that God made both the seen and the unseen. What are some of the unseen things?

(Wind, outer space, viruses, atoms, spiritual beings, etc.)

5. How might these verses from Colossians help someone who's afraid that everything is falling apart and that God no longer has any power in the world?

(God is still in control in spite of the condition of the world around us. Since God created everything [earthly and spiritual powers], for and through Christ, we should have no fear, for God rules over everything.)

6. How could you use Ephesians 3:20 and Philippians 4:13 to support the answer you gave above?

(Not only does God's power continue to work in the world, but His power actually works through the Holy Spirit within those who love Him.)

Discuss the following questions after you've completed "God Power."

What analogy does Jesus use in Matthew 7:7-11 to help us understand how we can plug into God's power?

(Jesus talks about asking, seeking, and knocking on a door, all of which encourage us to tell God about our needs; Jesus says God will respond lovingly and generously, even more than a loving, earthly father would to his own child.)

How do we know we can trust God to answer our prayers?

(Two reasons: God loves us, and He is all-powerful and all-knowing. A loving Father who has the power is certainly going to meet all our needs.)

Have kids, using the backs of their "God Power" sheets, write summaries of what a person has to do to take advantage of the power available from God. Let volunteers read their summaries.

We've seen that God is a sustainer and the all-powerful Creator who offers His unlimited resources to us. Let's see how that power still applies today.

3 POSSESSING THE POWER

Goal: That your students will begin to draw on the power God offers us.

Distribute copies of Action Sheet 7B to your kids and have them read the quote from Ralph Waldo Emerson: "All I have seen teaches me to trust the Creator for all I have not seen."

Then discuss the questions below.

What does this statement mean to you?

How might seeing God working in nature help you trust Him in other areas of life?

What are some things you have seen in the lives of Christians you know that cause you to trust God's power?

If kids seem hesitant to respond, mention a few things you have seen that help you trust in God's power. Then encourage kids to do the same.

What are some unseen things (problems, concerns) kids need to trust God to help with?

The power of God is available to each of us. God wants us to plug into His great power source.

We come up against a lot of difficult problems, and without God's power, we're in big trouble. It's not easy to be totally honest when kids all around are cheating. It's awfully hard not to tell white lies and often those a shade darker. It's impossible to handle our problems successfully without God's help. And God is always there to help.

Think of an area in which you need God's power—maybe a problem coming up or a situation you face often. If you really believe God's power can help you and you want to seek His help, write down a sentence prayer expressing your request.

Give kids a few minutes to write their prayers. **Then say: It's comforting to know that the same God that scattered the galaxies through space and formed massive mountain ranges makes His power available to us.**

Close your class by having volunteers read their sentence prayers aloud or simply ask God to help them remember and use His power in the coming week.

An Everlasting Love

SESSION 8 | 41

Session Aim

That your students will realize that God wants a personal, loving relationship with them, and that their lives would be incomplete without God's presence.

Key Verse

The Lord appeared to us in the past, saying: "I have loved you with an everlasting love; I have drawn you with loving-kindness" (Jeremiah 31:3).

Things You'll Need

- *Paper, pencils*
- *Bibles*
- *"What If . . ." (Action Sheet 8A)*
- *"Why Are We Here?" (Action Sheet 8B)*
- *Chalkboard and chalk*
- *Worship choruses*

***Distorted views of God abound.** Cult members aren't the only people who have mistaken ideas about who God is; Christians can misunderstand His nature, too.*

For example, some Christian teens—and adults—find it hard to believe that God really loves them personally. They need to understand that God is personal—that He cares about each one of us and wants us to have fellowship with Him.

In this session, you'll explore the personal nature of God and see how He seeks to have a relationship with each one of us. As you teach, you can help your kids develop a loving relationship with the God who loves them so much that He sent His Son to die for their sins.

1
THE BILLBOARD

Goal: That your students will begin to think about why God created humans.

Pass out copies of "What If . . ." (Action Sheet 8A) to your kids as they arrive. Have them think about the Scripture statement at the top of the sheet. When you're ready to start your session, have kids work on the question below the Scripture.

Suppose this statement were plastered in huge letters on a billboard beside a busy highway. What kinds of reactions would people have as they drove by and saw it?

Have each of your kids come up with at least six different reactions to list on the sheet. If kids have trouble coming up with reactions, ask them to think about how the following viewers might respond: a pastor, a college art student, an engineer, a newspaper reporter, a high school football player, and a person recently divorced. When kids are ready, have volunteers tell what reactions they came up with, and have them tell a little bit about the persons they think might have each reaction.

For example, a person in advertising might look at the billboard and say, "What a waste of good advertising space." This person might have some hazy belief about God, but doesn't think that God affects his or her life at all.

After all your volunteers have shared, lead into the next section by asking kids how they would respond to the people they've just talked about.

If you were able to talk to some of these people about the billboard, what would you say?

Let kids make suggestions. Then conclude the discussion with a comment like this:

We as Christians know the answer to the question, "Where did man come from?" God created us. But there are still some tough questions left to tackle. In today's lesson we'll discuss just one of them: "Why am I here?" No one can find real purpose in life until he or she finds the reason we were created.

2 YES, BUT WHY?

Goal: That your students will discover through a study of Scripture that God created them for fellowship with Him.

Distribute copies of "Why Are We Here?" (Action Sheet 8B), and have kids go through it individually. When they are finished, discuss their answers. The study is reprinted for you with additional discussion questions and some possible answers.

God created us. We know that. But why did He create us? Let's look at some Scripture to find out.

1. Read Genesis 1:26-28. In the space below, draw a diagram using symbols, lines, and words which illustrates the most important thing you learn in this passage about our relationship with God.

(Kids will probably draw something indicating that humans were created in God's image.)

How are humans in the "image of God"? What do humans have that the rest of the created creatures don't have?

(Humans have a "self," which can both remember and project into the future. We are free, moral beings—able to make decisions. People can be rational and intelligent. We are capable of love. Our souls are immortal. We are capable of ruling the earth.)

2. The fact that God created us in His own image suggests that God created us like Him so that we could relate to Him in some way. Read Ephesians 1:3-5. What kind of relationship did God have in mind when He created people?

(God wanted us as His sons and daughters in a loving, giving relationship or fellowship. He wants us to be holy before Him in love—that is, to maintain the image in which He created us—so that we may be in close fellowship with Him.)

3. Although humans were created in God's image, they have since fallen away into sin. Read Romans 1:21-23; Ephesians 2:1-3; Colossians 1:21. In what ways has sin spoiled our fellowship with God?

(Because of sin, man doesn't always give God the honor due Him; man ends up worshiping idols instead of

God, thus cutting off possibilities for relating to God. When we sin, we become spiritually less sensitive. We become "dead" in our sins and miss out on a relationship with God entirely. If we continue in sin, we grow farther away from our Holy God. And if we persist in our sinning, we actually become His enemies.)

How have communications been hurt, not only between humans and God, but between men and women on earth? How have our relationships lost the ideal of Genesis 1:26-28; 2:24?

(After sin entered the world, men and women could no longer live together in perfect harmony, jointly ruling the earth. Both men and women want to go their own directions, and refuse to submit to each other and to God.)

4. How can we be sure that God continues to reach out to us in love even though we have spoiled our relationship with Him through sin?

(We can be sure of God's continued love for us because, out of love, He reaches out to us through His Son. He has bridged the gap between people and Himself through Jesus' death on the cross.)

5. How does Acts 17:24-27 provide further evidence that God continues to seek fellowship with us?

(These verses show that God has no practical need for people, yet He still wants us to seek fellowship with Him: He is not far away if only we'll look for Him.)

6. God's purpose in creating us was that we might have fellowship with Him. Why do you think the God of all the universe was interested in fellowship with us? Read Jeremiah 31:3 and find out.

(God loves us.)

What can we do to respond to God's desire for fellowship with us? See John 4:13-21 for some help.

(We must want to be close to Him and live so that sin doesn't interfere. And if we truly have the Spirit of God within us, we will show His love to others. We must commit our lives to Jesus Christ, the Savior of the world.)

It really doesn't make sense to love apart from God's fellowship. God made us for a special reason—to continually communicate with Him. If we don't find that purpose, we won't experience real living.

If you have kids in your class who haven't accepted Christ, use the following paragraphs to encourage them to make a decision.

Jesus said, "I have come that they may have life, and have it to the full" (John 10:10b). Would you like the contentment that comes only from knowing you are doing the thing you were made for?

This is a serious decision. If you think you would like to have the Creator as Lord of your life, see me after we're finished and we'll talk further about how you can respond to God's love.

Be sure to be available after your session.

3 CLOSE TO YOU

Goal: That your students will identify specific situations in which they are able to feel God's presence in their lives.

The key points to be learned today are that God has created your kids for fellowship with Him and that their lives are incomplete without that fellowship. Toward that end, help kids evaluate their sense of closeness to the Lord. Have them take the following survey to discover when they most often feel God's presence.

I'm going to read a list of situations we've probably all experienced. As you think about each one, try to judge how often you feel God's presence, if you do, when you're in that situation.

Hand out sheets of paper and have kids number down the left side from 1 to 12. Tell kids *not* to put their names on this sheet.

We'll use a scale of one to five to grade each situation. Put a five if you "almost always" feel God's presence. Four will mean often; three, sometimes; two, seldom; and one, almost never. You may want to put this scale on the board.

When we are done, we'll tally up the class results and see where the "close spots" are—the situations where you feel God's presence most.

Here are the situations:

1. Listening to a class lecture in school
2. Sitting quiet and alone outside
3. Riding in a car
4. Talking to my parents
5. Listening to a sermon
6. Being with my friends
7. Eating lunch
8. Listening to a rock concert
9. Praying
10. Being at a football game
11. Singing a hymn
12. Looking at the stars

Ask kids to hand in their papers. Then have a couple of volunteers quickly add up the scores for each situation. Write the results on the board or read them.

Discuss the top two or three responses and why kids chose them. Also discuss the bottom responses. Then move on to the following questions.

Do you think we should feel God's presence more at certain times, or should we feel He's there all the time? Why?

(Maybe we *should* feel His constant presence, but there are very few people who would claim to have the same conscious awareness of His presence in all these situations.)

How much can we depend on feelings to know if God is there? Explain.

(Feelings are not always accurate. Indigestion or fatigue can make anyone feel poorly. God promises never to leave us if we trust Him. The important thing is that we know He is there, whether we feel Him or not.)

What kinds of activities can interfere with our fellowship with God?

(Sometimes we might not feel God's nearness because we know He doesn't want us to be where we are; have kids list some possible places. Other times, we make ourselves so busy we don't have time for God. If we forget Him, of course we won't feel His presence.)

It's exciting when we really take time to think about God's presence in us. The mighty God, the Creator, wants to communicate with us! Let's have a brief worship service right now. Let's thank God for His friendship, and catch the excitement of belonging to Him.

Have each of your kids write statements of praise and thanks to God, thanking Him for specific times when His presence meant a lot to them. Here are some examples to share with your kids: "Thank You, Lord, for allowing me to feel Your presence and love when I found out a friend had lied about me." "I praise you for giving me a more sensitive conscience, Lord, than I used to have."

Give kids a few minutes to prepare. Open the worship with a song; then give kids a chance to prayerfully present their praise to God. Also encourage kids to silently tell God things they didn't want to say aloud.

If your kids like to sing, close your session with a worshipful chorus, like "Alleluia" or "Father, I Adore You."

No Justice, Please

Session Aim

That your kids will understand that if God were only just and not merciful, none of us could please Him.

Key Verse

"As it is written: 'There is no one righteous, not even one.' Therefore no one will be declared righteous in his sight by observing the law; rather, through the law we become conscious of sin" (Romans 3:10, 20).

Things You'll Need

- *Paper, pencils*
- *Bibles*
- *Chalkboard and chalk, or newsprint and markers*
- *"State Your Case" (Action Sheet 9A)*
- *"What's the Word?" (Action Sheet 9B)*

We tend to demand justice—sometimes. *We want what is rightfully due us. We want those who have done wrong to be punished and those who have been wronged to be restored. But when it comes to facing God, demanding justice is not what we want. God's standard is perfection, and no human can measure up. So by the standard of justice, we're all condemned to death because of sin.*

Thank God the story doesn't end there! God, in His mercy, provided the sacrifice to satisfy His justice—His Son, Jesus Christ. Help your kids begin to thank God for the mercy He has shown everyone who believes in Him.

1 FILM AT ELEVEN

Goal: That your kids will come up with ideas to demonstrate the concept of justice.

What is justice? How would you define it for a group of children? Let's give it a try.

Divide your group into pairs. Each pair is to plan a movie for children illustrating what justice is. Any type of film the pairs want to plan is fine: cartoon, documentary, drama, musical, or whatever they think would best communicate the concept of justice to elementary kids.

Pairs should brainstorm what scenes and story lines they could include. Allow about five minutes before groups share what they have developed.

Which film idea sounds like it would best teach little kids about justice? Why? What would you have to do to add a definition of mercy to your film? How is mercy related to justice?

Of course God didn't make a film to teach us about justice and mercy, but we do have His Book which contains all we have to know about them. We're going to talk about being just and merciful, and how those words describe two important things about God.

2 JUSTICE ON TRIAL

Goal: That your students will study Scriptures to help them write definitions of God's justice and mercy.

Now, acting as law students, your class will evaluate the case presented in "State Your Case" (Action Sheet 9A). Distribute "State Your Case" and have your kids work in pairs on part 1A of the sheet. The questions from the sheet are printed for you here, along with additional questions and possible answers.

State Your Case

Fill in the data below, first on God the Judge and then on the guilty person. Base any observations or conclusions on the evidence from Scripture.

1. The Judge

A. How do the following verses illustrate to you that God is just and is determined to seek justice?

Genesis 6:5-7

(When God saw that man had violated His standards of perfection, He was determined to destroy man. According to God's justice, those who break a commandment deserve to be punished for it.)

Romans 3:23-26

(In these verses God demonstrates His justice in that He demands some payment for the crime which has been committed—man's sin. As Paul says, the payment made was Christ Himself. In this way God's justice is affirmed.)

Psalm 98:8, 9

(According to the writer of the psalm, all of creation rejoices at the prospect that God will judge people equally, with justice.)

Revelation 6:17

(God is not going to let people get away with their sin. His justice will stand in the end, just as it stands today.)

Stop at this point and go over kids' answers. Then pass out copies of "What's the Word?" (Action Sheet 9B). Have kids discuss the definition of justice on the sheet and then work on definitions of their own, using their own ideas and the Scriptures they've studied so far. Use a chalkboard or newsprint and have one student act as a scribe to write down your kids' joint definition of God's justice. Be sure the scribe leaves half of the board or sheet for another definition.

"God's justice makes the need for His mercy obvious." Does your definition of God's justice make sense in relation to what I just read?

(Read the statement again, then let kids respond. Kids should have understood that God does not compromise in His justice. Therefore, those who are imperfect in their behavior deserve to be punished. The only reason humans have hope is that God is also merciful.)

Now work through part 1 B of "State Your Case."

B. How do the following verses illustrate to you that God is merciful?

Genesis 6:8, 9

(These verses show us that even though God saw the wickedness of man, He was willing to show mercy to a man who walked with Him. God would have been justified in destroying the human race, but He allowed it to continue.)

Romans 3:23-26; 5:8, 9

(Even though people sinned and came short of God's glory, God in His mercy was willing to justify man freely through Christ Jesus.)

Now have your kids look back at the definition of mercy on "What's the Word?" Using that definition and the Scripture they've studied, have your kids write a definition for God's mercy. Have your scribe add it to the chalkboard or newsprint.

Kids should see that God's mercy involves withholding punishment even when justice demands it.

How does this concept of God's mercy make you feel?

How can God be both just and merciful at the same time?

(God didn't overlook sin. The punishment had to be paid to maintain God's justice. But in His mercy, God took the punishment upon Himself through His Son Jesus Christ. Anyone accepting that substitution receives the merciful pardon from what justice demands.)

Now work on parts 2 and 3 of "State Your Case." You may want to have kids work in pairs or small groups.

2. The Client

A. What's the person's crime? Look at Genesis 6:5-7; Romans 1:21, 32; 3:10-12, 20, 23.

Assign a different verse to each group or student.

(The person's crime is sin. People are filled with wickedness and their thoughts are evil; they ignore God and His laws and do not glorify Him.)

Have a student read the definition of sin from "What's the Word?" to help kids define what crime humankind has committed.

How do these verses and the definition help you understand why God can't tolerate sin?

What do these verses about sin tell you about God's justice?

(Humans are guilty when they stand before God's justice. We have sinned against His laws, and nothing we can do can satisfy the demands of His justice. His justice is far beyond even our best standards of following the law or doing what is right.)

B. What if the person says, "I didn't know any better"? What kind of answer could you give him or her? See Romans 1:19, 20.

(Ignorance is no excuse. God has made Himself visible through Creation and His plan clear through His Word and His followers. If a person searches, God will show him or her the truth.)

Since God knew from the beginning that man would sin, why did He make man with the capacity for disobedience?

Since Scripture doesn't answer this question directly, we can only speculate. Show your students some of the following principles we do know.

People were created in the image of God, and the freedom to act is one of God's attributes. Humans are like God in their capacity to make moral choices.

God wanted to enter into personal, loving relationships with people. He loves them and wants to be loved in return. This could only be done if people were free to decide whether or not to love God.

Are we responsible for our acts of sin? Don't heredity and environment determine our behavior? Explain your answer.

The problem with this view is that it could become an excuse for any behavior—murder, torture, robbery, or anything. Punishment is meaningless unless people are held responsible for their actions.

The Bible says God gave us the ability to choose between right and wrong. He naturally holds us responsible for the choices we make. God gave us the gifts of intelligence and moral choice. Unfortunately, everyone misuses those gifts.

3. Conclusions

A. Assume this person is brought to trial. As you see what kind of judge God is and as you look over the person's case, what verdict do you think is possible? Explain.

(If the person is content in his or sins, then because God is a just God, the verdict would be guilty. This is punishable by death according to Romans 6:23. However, as we have seen, God is also merciful. If the person is willing to repent of his or her sins and receive redemption through Christ, then the verdict would be not guilty.)

B. Suppose the person signs into the court record his or her testimony that he or she is personally committed to the truth of Romans 3:23, 24. How does this affect the verdict?

(Through God's mercy, the person is justified. He or she will not be required to pay the penalty. The verdict will be "innocent.")

C. How does this demonstrate the importance of God's mercy?

(According to God's perfect standard of justice, anyone who lives with less than perfect behavior is condemned by the law. It is only by means of God's mercy through Christ that we have a chance to be saved from the guilty verdict.)

D. If you had to come before the Judge with your own case, which verdict would you receive? On what basis would you plead for mercy?

Have kids give brief testimonies of what they feel Christ has done for them. Those who have accepted Christ recently can especially point out how they can plead for mercy on the basis of what Christ did on the cross.

3 THANK GOD FOR MERCY!

Goal: That your students will thank God for the mercy He shows us.

If God judged us by the same standards by which we often judge others, there wouldn't be much hope of ever measuring up. Fortunately, God adds mercy to His justice. If you would like to talk more about discovering what God, in His mercy, has done for you, come see me after class.

Those of us who already have benefited from God's mercy need to thank God for that mercy and learn to show that kind of mercy to others.

Close your session in prayer, guiding kids' prayers with the following thoughts:

1. Thank God for His gift of salvation to you.

2. Think of one specific thing for which God has forgiven you. Thank Him for His mercy to you.

3. Think of an area in your life where you might not be totally pleasing Him. Ask for His forgiveness, His mercy. Promise with His help to change. Then thank Him.

Depend on Him

Session Aim

That your students will appreciate God's dependability in the midst of a constantly changing world.

Key Verse

"Every good and perfect gift is from above, coming down from the Father of the heavenly lights, who does not change like shifting shadows" (James 1:17).

Things You'll Need

* *Paper, pencils*
* *Bibles*
* *"God Is . . ." (Action Sheet 10A)*
* *"Give Me a Hundred Men" (Action Sheet 10B)*

Think your world is changing too quickly? *In a teenager's world, things generally change even more rapidly. New fads and fashions replace old ones too quickly for most adults to keep track. Boyfriends and girlfriends can be dropped so frequently that some kids can't plan their lives more than a few days in advance.*

Change creates anxiety. Remember the last time you faced a major change? The changes kids face may seem minor to us, but those upheavals may be the biggest ones they've ever encountered.

"Praise the Lord, He never changes." These words from a song of a few years ago capture the essence of this session. We all need a solid, constant base for our lives. Help your kids depend on the God who will never change—the God who will be the same tomorrow as He was 3,000 years ago!

1 RULES AND THE RULER

Goal: That your students will see God as the unchanging basis be-

hind the similar laws found in all cultures.

Have your kids look up Malachi 3:6 and read it aloud. Then divide the class into three different groups. Your groups will represent different types of cultures. Assign the following three cultures to your groups: Tribal, Medieval, and Technological.

Give each group the description below that pertains to that group.

Tribal
1. Small groups, sometimes separated by miles
2. Hunting and fishing as main occupations
3. Extensive family closeness, kinship
4. Closeness to nature in religion
5. A dominant fear of the unknown

Medieval
1. Feudal lord and serf relationship
2. Little chance for advancement
3. Much agriculture
4. External allegiance of many to the church
5. Little concern for any sort of political activity

Technological
1. Much of the labor done by machines
2. Fast transportation and the tendency to change locations often
3. Families just parent or parents and children
4. Optimism about scientific achievement
5. Increase in psychological problems

Ask each group to set up five rules it thinks should govern its society's behavior. Encourage your kids to discuss among themselves what they've learned at school about societies like these.

After the groups have formed their behavioral rules, ask: **In what ways were your rules similar?**

(If kids approached this project seriously, their rules should cover some of the basic laws which society today uses to govern itself. Help students see that common laws about what is right and wrong in society are due to our common humanity. Even though cultural situations vary, many moral and social problems are universal.)

How would you explain the fact that society has universal laws?

(They are obviously the best way to operate even from a merely human perspective, and were set by the same God who decided right and wrong. He is the Person behind the rules which people of all times accept as morally right.)

2 HERE TODAY, HERE TOMORROW

Goal: That your students will study several passages of Scripture and report on the characteristics of God they find there.

It's time to set your students loose in Scripture to discover for themselves that God is unchanging. Use whatever method works best for your group to go through this study.

Pass out copies of "God Is . . ." (Action Sheet 10A) and have your kids work on the assignments there. The assignments and Scriptures from the Action Sheet, some suggested answers, and additional questions are given here.

Use the following Scripture texts to create a list of characteristics that describe what God is like. Some characteristics will be obvious from the text; others you can assume based on what the text tells you about God. Underline the attributes that were true at the time the Scripture was written and are still true of God today.

1. Malachi 3:6

"I the Lord do not change. So you, O descendants of Jacob, are not destroyed."

Don't limit yourself or your students to the following answers, but use them as a starting point. Students should underline every attribute of God they find, since each applied when the Scripture was written and each applies today.

Some possible answers:

God is powerful. The word *Lord* assumes His leadership and absolute power.

God is unchanging. Obviously this is a focus of today's session. It's easy to find in the text, but make certain that kids verbalize it as you go over the Malachi passage.

God appears to be merciful. Although we can't tell from this single verse, we get the feeling that if He weren't merciful, the sons of Jacob would have been destroyed.

God has a relationship with people. He is directly involved with the sons of Jacob. Some students might carry the point further by saying that *God is personal.*

2. Exodus 20:1-3

"And God spoke all these words: 'I am the Lord your God, who brought you out of Egypt, out of the land of slavery. You shall have no other gods before me.' "

Don't let your students whip through this assignment, finding only the most obvious characteristics. Press them to dig a little. Prod them with questions like "What do you think a scholar who spent three days on these verses might discover?"

Here are some possible answers. You will probably want to do your own inductive study of the passage in addition to considering the following:

God is personal. This was hinted at in the previous passage, but here He is actually talking with people.

God is powerful. These sentences are orders. He tells His people who He is and then He lays down the law. There is no room for guessing what He means. The words are simple and their meaning is not to be questioned.

God loves His people. This is based on the fact that He did good things for His people by taking them out of Egypt. It's a guess from this passage, but of course, this fact is confirmed in other passages.

God is involved in the events of history.

This is a function rather than a characteristic. It might be said that God is the *prime mover.* He controls history.

God is demanding. We often say this of a person in a negative sense, but it doesn't have to be. God has established His concern and His protection of His people. He has every right to expect His people to respect and obey Him. He doesn't hesitate to let them know it.

God is jealous. Again, this is a positive, rather than a negative, statement. God is the only God, and He insists that His people acknowledge that. He will not share His time with any man-made gods.

God is protective. The Egyptian example proves this, but we also see it in God's use of the word *your.* He is telling them that they belong to Him and He belongs to them.

3. Psalm 99: 2-5

"Great is the Lord in Zion; he is exalted over all the nations. Let them praise your great and awesome name—he is holy. The King is mighty, he loves justice—you have

established equity; in Jacob you have done what is just and right. Exalt the Lord our God and worship at his footstool; he is holy."

(Some possible answers: The Lord is great; the Lord is supreme; the Lord is just; the Lord is righteous.)

When you've gone over your kids' responses for all the passages, have them think about all the characteristics they saw. Then say something like this: **Based on the words you've underlined, make one observation about God.**

Kids should have underlined all the characteristics of God they found. Their observations should include the fact that God is the same now as He was when these verses were written.

Our God doesn't change, and His standards for His people don't change. What are some of God's changeless standards?

(General principles of right and wrong, the Ten Commandments, etc.)

Name some Biblical characters who acted on God's standards even though they could have avoided physical harm by ignoring them.

(Daniel, Stephen, Paul, many others.)

If we could save ourselves some grief by disregarding God's laws once in a while, why not do it?

(Don't let kids get away with pat answers on this one. Encourage them to think about it. Help them to admit the difficulty that obeying God sometimes brings.)

Look at James 1:17. How does it relate to what we've been talking about? How can this verse reassure us that not only is God's moral law good for us, but that it is unchanging?

(Everything that God does for us, especially setting up His moral law, is good for us. He gives us the moral law as He gives us gifts because He loves us. Furthermore, we can be certain that He will not change the rules on us.)

3 BLESSED ASSURANCE

Goal: That your students will understand how God's unchanging nature assures us that we can depend on Him.

Pass out copies of Action Sheet 10B and have kids read the quote on the sheet. Then say something like this:

We, as Christians, are committed to living according to God's unchanging laws. But some of us don't do such a great job. In fact, John Wesley would probably have a difficult

time finding 100 people who would hate sin and nothing else, and fear God and nothing else.

I want to be one of those people God will use to change the world, and maybe you do, too. John Wesley's statement can help remind you about God's unchanging standards, and can help you remember to fear God and hate sin. The more we pattern our lives after Jesus Christ and His living example, the more God will be able to use us—to change our lives, our communities, our schools, and maybe even our world.

Tell us about someone you think might fit into the group of 100 Wesley was talking about. How is that person following God's changeless standards? How is that person changing his or her part of the world for God?

How do you think knowing that God is unchanging helps this person serve God better?

These last two questions challenge kids to think of other Christians they respect. Adults can become human models of how Christianity can be lived in a constantly changing world. Of course, these models are imperfect, but kids need to see that growth doesn't end when you become an adult.

Even the most committed Christians make mistakes. But our unchanging God doesn't.

If God were not unchanging and dependable, what might happen?

(Let kids turn their imaginations loose on the possibilities. For example, if God were not dependable, His creation might not be either; the law of gravity might not apply every day, and we'd go sailing into space. Or God might not always be available to hear our requests. He could break His promises, change His laws, and decide to turn His back on us—all without notice.)

After considering these possibilities, close your class in prayer. Ask volunteers to thank God for specific attributes, and for His unchanging love.

SESSION 11   TRUE TO HIS WORD   56

Session Aim

To help your kids gain confidence in God's power to keep all His promises.

Key Verses

"Yet he did not waver through unbelief regarding the promise of God, but was strengthened in his faith and gave glory to God, being fully persuaded that God had power to do what he had promised" (Romans 4:20, 21).

Things You'll Need

- *Bibles*
- *Pencils*
- *"No Laughing Matter" (Action Sheet 11A)*
- *"Practicing the Promises" (Action Sheet 11B)*

God makes a lot of promises. Unlike many of us, however, He never makes them lightly. Nor does He stop with seriousness and good intentions; He always keeps His promises.

His record is overwhelming. Old Testament prophecies fulfilled in the New Testament, for example, are enough to convince all but the most skeptical critic. God is a loving God, so He wants to keep His promises to us. He is also an all-powerful God, so He is able to keep those promises.

Use this session to help your kids trust more in the promises of God. Help them see that what God has promised will happen, and that He wants to give the benefits of His promises to the people who love Him.

1 PROMISES, PROMISES

Goal: That your students will understand the meaning of the word, "promise."

Ask:

Have you ever made a promise? Has anyone ever made a promise to you?

What is one recent promise which concerned you?

Let kids respond and tell about their experiences.

Now, imagine that you have a visitor from another planet. He hears you say something about a promise and asks you what you mean. How are you going to explain what it means to promise?

Allow time for your kids to define the word, then check a dictionary for a definition. Webster's Seventh New Collegiate Dictionary says that "promise" comes from a Latin word meaning "to send forth." It is a declaration that you will do, or will not do, a specific thing. It is frequently made to a particular person, and gives that person the right to expect that you will do as you have said.

Most people understand that when one says he or she will do something, that person is promising to do whatever he says he will do. Other people say, "I promise" with no intention of doing what they have promised.

Sometimes people make promises with every intention of keeping their word, but are unable to, because of some factor they have no power to control.

One thing we can be sure of: God is always faithful to His word. God keeps His promises no matter what. Because He is Truth itself, God will always do what He has promised.

Because He is God, and all-powerful, no circumstances can prevent Him from doing so.

Today we're going to look at how Abram, now called Abraham, learned this truth about God.

2 HE WHO LAUGHS LAST . . .

Goal: That your students will study a Biblical example and discuss what it teaches about God's promises.

To give kids the whole story behind today's session, have them read Genesis 18:1-14 and 21:5.

Pass out copies of "No Laughing Matter" (Action Sheet 11A) and have a couple of good readers alternate reading paragraphs aloud.

When they're finished reading, divide your class into two groups to answer the following questions. A person in the group may answer only once until everyone else has also answered. You may want to keep score.

Award:

100 points for a perfect, complete answer;

60 points for most of the answer;

20 points for a wrong answer which

the group is able to correct after consultation.

Kids may refer to their Bibles or to "No Laughing Matter" at any time.

The questions and possible answers are given for you here. You might want to set a time limit, like one minute, for finding answers.

Group 1: Who were Abraham's visitors by the trees of Mamre? Check Genesis 18 and 19:1.

(Genesis 18:1 says the Lord appeared to Abraham. Verse 2 speaks of three men. From the rest of the chapter and 19:1, we can gather that the three were the Lord and two angels, in human forms.)

Group 2: What was the purpose of their coming?

(Verses 10 and 14 make it clear that the Lord came to remove any doubt of His promise of a son to Abraham and Sarah.)

Group 1: Was this the first Abraham and Sarah had heard of this coming event? See Genesis 17:15-22.

(It seems to have been the first Sarah had heard of it. According to Genesis 17, God had previously made it known to Abraham.)

Group 2: What had been Abraham's reaction at first? See Genesis 17:17, 18.

(Doubt and skepticism. He had laughed, expressed disbelief that he and Sarah could conceive a child, and suggested that the covenant might be fulfilled through Ishmael, his son by the servant Hagar.)

Group 1: Why do you suppose Abraham came to accept God's promise of Isaac? See Genesis 12:1, 5; 17:5, 19.

(Ever since he had left Haran, Abraham had been in the process of learning that God was dependable. God had come with him, and brought him safely out of Haran. God had promised him the land of Canaan, and he was now in it.)

Furthermore, God had given Abraham two reminders of the new relationship which existed between them (Genesis 17). The first was a new name. Abram was now Abraham, "father of many nations," or "father of a multitude." The second was the rite of circumcision, a visible symbol of the fact that Abraham and all his household now belonged to God.

All of these things must have assured Abraham that he had no reason not to believe God!

Group 2: What was Sarah's reaction to the promise that she would have a baby? Why?

(She, like Abraham at first, laughed in disbelief because she knew that she was humanly incapable of conceiving a child. Instead of looking at what God had already done, she was looking at her own limitations.)

Group 1: How did God respond to Sarah's doubt?

(As recorded in Genesis 18:14, He directed Abraham's attention—and Sarah's, too, because she was still listening at the tent door—away from Sarah's ability and toward His own: "Is anything too hard for the Lord?")

Group 2: Turn to Genesis 21:1-7. How did this incident end?

(God was true to His word. He did for Sarah what He had said He would do, when He had said He would do it.)

Abraham, remembering his own and Sarah's disbelieving laughter, named his baby son Isaac, meaning "he laughs." Sarah, who a year before had laughed skeptically, now laughed for joy in God's faithfulness, and her delight in having the new baby she had wanted for so many years.

Sarah's words in Genesis 21:6 express so much happiness they could almost be a poem or a song:

"God has brought me laughter, and everyone who hears about this will laugh with me."

Group 1: Was the birth of Isaac a miracle?

(Since it was humanly impossible for a woman who has passed her years of fertility to conceive a child, and since Sarah, at age 75, could hardly have been mistaken about her condition, we must call the birth of Isaac a miracle.)

Webster's New World Dictionary of the American Language defines "miracle" as follows: "An event or action that apparently contradicts known scientific laws and hence [is] thought to be due to supernatural causes, especially to an act of God."

Group 2: What does this teach us about God?

(God, who is the Source of all natural laws, has the power to change or suspend those laws when it is necessary for His purposes.)

The greatest instances of God's setting aside natural laws were, of course, the virgin birth of Jesus Christ and His resurrection.

Remember God's word to Sarah, "Is anything too hard for the Lord?" Jesus said almost exactly the same thing when talking about a rich man's chances of being saved: "The things which are impossible with men are possible with God" (Luke 18:27, KJV).

Add the scores and announce the winning group.

Whether the obstacles are natural physical laws or conditions within people's hearts and minds, God has the power to keep His promises in spite of them.

Now, with a partner, look up the references given in the paragraph at the bottom of "No Laughing Matter," and answer the question.

Find the promises God makes in the

following verses and put a check beside those which have already come true. How do you know the others will also come true?

Genesis 3:15

John 14:26, 28

John 15:10

I John 2:25

John 14:2, 3

Discuss kids' answers, then move on to the final part of this session.

3 PROCLAIMING HIS PROMISES

Goal: That your students will find some of the promises made by God in Scripture and determine how they are to respond to them.

Although nothing is impossible with God, in what ways can we hinder God's promises from being fulfilled in our lives?

(Lack of faith, or unbelief; a failure to fulfill the conditions which are attached to the promise, or simply a failure to realize that the promise has been made, and that it applies to us.)

What does God expect from His people in response to His promises?

(Basically, He expects faith—belief that He will keep His word—and the performance of our part of the promise, whatever conditions are attached to it.)

Let's see how this works out with some promises God has made to us in His Word.

Pass out copies of "Practicing the Promises" (Action Sheet 11B). **We're going to look carefully at a few promises in Scripture. Look up the first reference on your sheet, and fill in the chart for that reference.**

Go through the chart one reference at a time, having kids report their answers before you move on to another reference. Proceed in a similar manner with all the references on the sheet. The references are printed for you here:

Romans 10:9

I John 1:9

Matthew 21:22

Exodus 20:12

Revelation 2:10

I John 3:22

Encourage your kids to share promises which God has fulfilled for them. You might start by telling about your salvation experience or an answer to prayer—perhaps one where the answer was "No" or "Wait." In that instance God kept His promise, but not as you would have wished.

Close your session by having the two groups who worked together write group prayers, thanking God for keeping His promises. Each group should choose one student to read his or her finished prayer to God.

HELP IS ON THE WAY!

Session Aim

That your students will seek God's involvement in the everyday ups and downs as well as the major crises of their lives.

Key Verse

"If that is how God clothes the grass of the field, which is here to-day and tomorrow is thrown into the fire, will he not much more clothe you, O you of little faith?" (Matthew 6:30).

Things You'll Need

- *Pencils, paper*
- *"Me?" (Action Sheet 12A)*
- *Bibles*
- *"Details! Details!" (Action Sheet 12B)*

Yes, God is all-powerful, all-knowing, eternal, and perfect. But is He available?

Or are God's ways so far above our ways that He is unapproachable? Is our awesome, almighty God too busy with cosmic problems to worry about the little things we face each day?

No! Amazingly, God is concerned about even the smallest of our problems. He is a Heavenly Father who cares about His earthly family. He's never unconcerned or too busy to help one of His children.

In this session, help your kids grasp the idea that God really does care about their problems—no matter how little those problems are. God wants us to depend on Him. We can call on God for help whenever we need it, and we know He'll always be there.

1 WHO CARES?

Goal: That your students will examine how different people look at life.

Pass out pencils and paper to your kids, then give the following instructions.

Try letting your imagination run freely for a few minutes. I'm going to read several descriptions of life which convey the way some people feel that life is meaningless. As I read them, think about the feelings you get when you hear the descriptions. Write down or draw symbols of your feelings. You could draw an expression on someone's face. You could draw a chain to show hopelessness, or a man on an island to convey loneliness.

Make sure kids understand your instructions, then read the following descriptions, pausing after each one to give kids time to write or draw.

1. A pompous lawyer in a famous novel says that he's going to take what he can get out of life because all he has to look forward to when he gets to Heaven is a dark room the shape of a coffin, filled with hundreds of spiders.

2. A French writer compared life to a character in Greek mythology. This character, Sisyphus, was condemned to roll a stone up a long hill. Every time he just about got to the top of the hill, he would slip. The stone would roll all the way back down the hill, and he would have to start all over again.

**3. One poet said that life was like

being in a deep pit, hanging by a thin rope at which a mouse was gnawing.

Have your kids explain their drawings or their descriptions of their feelings; then pass out copies of "Me?" (Action Sheet 12A).

Let's read the thoughts of a girl who seems to think she's caught in the kind of world described by the people we've just talked about. God lets her know how wrong she is.

Have your kids read "Me?" You might want to have two students read it aloud, having each read one part. The dialogue is reprinted for you here:

"Me?"

I mean, the universe is such a big place that our earth is a mere fly spot in space.

I have created you.

And with all the billions of people crowding our planet, I'm no more significant than a grain of sand on one of the ocean's beaches.

You are My child.

And with all the people who've lived in the centuries before me . . .

I have known you since before the day of your birth.

And all the people who'll live in the years after I'm gone . . .

You are precious to Me.

How could God possibly have time to give me any attention? Or even no-

tice me? He probably doesn't even know I exist!

I have created you and you are My child. You are as important to Me as anyone who has ever lived.

Me? Are you talking about me? Are you sure?

Give kids a minute to think about what was said, then move on to the next section.

Many of us have questions as this girl did. Let's look at some evidence to show us how much God does care.

2 LET ME GET THIS STRAIGHT

Goal: That your students will discover that God cares about every detail of His creation.

Pass out copies of "Details! Details!" (Action Sheet 12B). Have your kids work together on the first three parts of the study. Keep the discussion moving by using the additional questions given here.

Details! Details!

1. Read Genesis 1:11, 12, 24, 25. What characteristics or attributes of God do you find suggested in this description of Creation? Call them out as you find them.

(Write down the characteristics as your kids call them out. Possibilities include omnipotent, productive, resourceful, creative, imaginative, conscientious, caring, pleased with what He had created, meticulous, versatile, caring about detail, etc.)

What is the difference between the meaningless life portrayed by the writers in the last section and the life of a person who believes in Scripture?

(While the lives portrayed earlier were purposeless, a person who believes in Scripture has purpose and knows the concern of a loving God.)

Paraphrase the following:

According to the Bible, we live in a world that has purpose. What difference does that make to us as individuals? Why are we sometimes overwhelmed with feelings of meaninglessness? Let's see what the Bible says.

Have your kids work on the next section of Action Sheet 12B.

2. Now read Matthew 6:30-33. What feelings do you think people were having that prompted Jesus to say this?

(Worry over an economic situation, anxiety about feeding their families, concern over a drought, worried that Rome would increase taxes.)

Note that God isn't saying here that we sit back and lazily wait for Him to drop food into our mouths and clothes over our bodies. He is saying we shouldn't spend our valuable, short time on earth worrying about material things. We should trust Him instead and spend our time promoting His Kingdom. He may not provide all the things we think we want; but the God who flung the galaxies into space, designed and made the trees, and created everything from pandas to people, knows and cares and provides for the details in our lives.

Have your kids read Matthew 6:30 again.

If things are going badly, how does this verse help us know whether or not God is testing us or neglecting us?

(The key here is having the faith that God meant what He said when He promised that He is involved in our lives for our own good.)

3. How would knowing the answer to question 1 help eliminate some of the anxieties the people were feeling in question 2?

(If God is conscientious enough to care about the small details of His creation such as distinguishing between seed-bearing herbs and fruit-bearing trees or designing the marks of each animal, then He will certainly care for the needs of each person who asks Him for help.)

For question 4, divide your students into three groups—one for each reference. Then have your kids report their answers.

4. The actions of many people in the Bible made it clear that they understood and believed the truth Jesus stated in Matthew. Look up the

following references and tell how these people showed their faith that God could take care of details in their lives.

A. II Kings 4:1-7

(The wife of one of the sons of the prophets lost her husband; a creditor came to take her two sons as slaves. She went to Elisha for help, and he told her to take a small jar of oil and fill other vessels with it. She followed his directions; the vessels filled with oil, and she sold the oil to pay her debts. She demonstrated her faith in God by doing what Elisha had told her to do, and God provided the money she needed.)

B. Mark 5:25-34

(A woman who had been suffering from hemorrhages for 12 years showed her faith by reaching out and touching the garment of Christ even though Christ was surrounded by many others. God took care of her by healing her.)

C. Acts 7:57-60

Note: Stephen had just finished going through the history of the Jewish people in an effort to show the Jewish council that Jesus Christ was the Messiah.

(Stephen was stoned to death. His martyrdom introduced the persecu-tion which scattered the disciples through Samaria and Judea and eventually to the West. This fulfilled Christ's command to preach the Gospel beyond Jerusalem. If Stephen had not been stoned, the disciples might have clustered around Jerusalem instead of reaching out. Kids should not be expected to say that God rescued Stephen in the time of danger; after all, Stephen was stoned to death. But they can see that Stephen trusted God to accomplish His will through this event; Stephen was forgiving rather than vengeful. You may want to point out that sometimes God calls us to contribute to a cause that is far more important then our private needs; if we trust Him to know what is best, He will, as in Stephen's case, give strength and peace even during suffering.)

Obviously C is different from A and B in that from a human standpoint God did not guide in the way we would wish. Yet Stephen gave first place to God's Kingdom and trusted God to take care of the details of his eternal life!

Have kids work on part 5 individually.

5. Think of a person you know who lives as if he or she understands and believes the truth Jesus stated in the Matthew verses. List several ways he or she has shown faith that God could take care of the details of his or her life.

After your kids have completed this section, have a few volunteers read their lists aloud. Be sure to do this exercise yourself, too.

3 SEEKING HIS HELP

Goal: That your students will identify specific problems in their lives and will seek God's help as they need it.

Think of some problems in your life which God could help you with. They could be huge or tiny. Remember, God is interested in us, His creation! He wants to be part of every area of our lives.

Have kids look at the "Task Calendar" at the bottom of Action Sheet 12B. Kids should fill in the chart with an item to work on each day. Each item should be something personal that is a problem for that person. Give kids a few suggestions such as "Try not to argue with Mom," "Get homework done early," and "Don't get angry with my little brother."

Encourage kids to begin each day by asking God to take part in every area of their lives. They should especially ask Him to help them with the problem for that day.

At the bottom of the chart, kids should describe how God helped them resolve the problem. Or if they messed up by not letting God take charge, they should write what they think God wants them to learn from the failure.

Suggest that kids pray for each other and maybe call a friend during the week to see how he or she is doing on the problems listed.

Have your kids close your session with prayer—praise and thanks to God for promising help with their problems, and requests for His daily help.

THE RIGHT TRACK

Session Aim

That your students will accept the correction of God as a necessary part of spiritual growth.

Key Verse

"For as high as the heavens are above the earth, so great is his love for those who fear him" (Psalm 103:11).

Things You'll Need

- *Paper, pencils*
- *Bibles*
- *"Will I Ever Learn, Lord?" (Action Sheet 13A)*
- *"Spiritual Growth" flowchart (Action Sheet 13B)*

***In the previous session your students learned that God is personally concerned about meeting their needs.** But meeting people's needs doesn't always mean granting their wants. Sometimes people need things they don't want at the moment—like correction.*

God isn't a Santa Claus who gives us goodies and a smile and then flies off into the sky. God wants us to grow spiritually, to become more like His Son. That kind of change often requires that God correct us.

Being corrected can be painful, but God's correction is never cruel. On the contrary, His correction is compassionate, merciful, and loving. Like a parent's warning not to play in the street, it can save us far more anguish than it causes.

Your kids may be open to God's involvement in their lives only so long as He sticks to granting their requests for safety, dates, and good grades. If so, they have a warped view of God. They need to know the rest of the story—His goal of keeping them on the right track. Seeing that side of God's nature may be the beginning of growth for some of your students, as they learn to expect and accept His compassionate, infinitely wise correction.

1

POETIC JUSTICE

Goal: That your students will read a poem to focus on how God corrects those who do wrong.

Begin your session by distributing copies of "Lord, Will I Ever Learn?" (Action Sheet 13A). Have a student read the poem aloud, if you have a good reader. Then discuss the following questions:

What does this poem tell you about the way God corrects those who've done wrong?

(Several answers are possible. For example, God "speaks" through our consciences; He is often more patient with us than we are with others; His correction is not necessarily the same as punishment; He shows us by example how we should act.)

How do you think the poet will react to God's correction?

(Answers may vary widely. Some possibilities: She will feel guilty; she will apologize to God; she will confess her sinful attitude; she will seek to be more patient with others, as God is with her.)

2 CORRECTION AND MERCY

Goal: That your students will study Scriptures to demonstrate that God's correction is purposeful and compassionate.

Pass out pencils and have your kids work individually or in pairs on part 1 of the study after the poem. When they have finished this part, go over their answers. Suggested answers and supplementary questions are included below.

Correction!

God's correction of humans is sometimes necessary. Let's see how He goes about correcting people who have done wrong.

1. When Adam and Eve ate the fruit from the forbidden tree, they disobeyed God and deserved to be punished.

In Genesis 3 we have a vivid picture of how God goes about punishing or correcting those who have sinned against Him.

A question comes up: What qualities does God show as He corrects His people?

Read through the references below and answer the question above for each reference.

A. Genesis 3:8-13

(Though God knows very well what Adam and Eve have done, He asks them patient questions about their version of the story. In this way He gets them to admit their own sin. He also wants us to face the truth about ourselves. In this way He demonstrates His fairness, patience, and compassion.)

B. Genesis 3:14, 15

Your kids may have some trouble with this one. You may have to help them out by giving them the next two paragraphs of information.

These verses show that God's correction can be sure, swift, and terrible. The serpent's punishment is equal to the seriousness of what it has done. God shows His justice here. He wants us to know that He is not soft-hearted and will not let anybody get off "scot-free."

Yet already, for humans, we begin to see God's mercy at work in verse 15. Here God promises to defeat Satan through a descendant of the woman, but in the process Satan will inflict harm on the descendant. This prophecy looks forward to Christ's crucifixion, where though He was "bruised" on the "heel," by dying, Christ rose from the dead and "bruised" the serpent's "head" by victoriously crushing Satan's power forever.

C. Genesis 3:16-19

(In these verses God describes the consequences of sin. Woman will have pain in childbirth, and man will eat all the days of his life in sorrow.

Again, we see that God is not compromising in the way He responds to sin.)

D. Genesis 3:21

(God made clothes out of skins for Adam and Eve, which shows God's compassion. He still loved them and provided for their needs even after they had disobeyed Him.)

E. Genesis 3:22-24

(In a way, casting Adam and Eve out of the Garden was a loving and merciful thing to do. Adam and Eve, now sinful people, would have been miserable living in a place of perfection. Another point of mercy here is that by banishing them from the Garden, God kept them from eating of the tree of life. Had they eaten from that tree, they would have lived eternally in their misery.)

Before going further in the Bible study, be sure to discuss kids' answers. Kids should begin to see a pattern both of God's purpose in correcting man's sin and of His compassion. These will come out further in the study of the Romans passage below.

2. Writing in Romans, Paul adds to the picture we have of God. From what Paul says, why do you think it was necessary for God to "correct" humans for their sins? See Romans 1:18, 21-23; 5:12.

Have different students take turns reading these verses from Romans.

After each verse, stop and discuss how the verse might help to answer the question.

(These verses show us that we have a God who cannot tolerate unrighteousness. Because of His perfect standard, He had to punish those who were filled with godlessness, who did not glorify Him as God or give thanks to Him, and who thought they had all the answers in themselves. In God's eyes this kind of wisdom was only foolishness. Paul also points to their idolatry, which was intolerable to God. God had to "correct" humans for their sins. Death was the punishment.)

Kids might find it helpful to look at a modern version of these verses.

In Romans 1:24, 26, 28, Paul says, "God gave them over" to their evil desires. Why did God do this? What does this mean?

(God had to let people see for themselves that they were slaves to sin and could never be free on their own. People may enjoy sin for a while, but when they want to quit, they find they can't. Sin breeds complete self-centeredness, and people who live only to satisfy themselves will never find contentment. Hopefully they will someday discover that only God can save them from their sins.)

Mankind, as described by Paul in these verses, is spiritually dead. There is nothing we can do about it ourselves. That's why God had to step in.

3. Read Romans 5:6-11. Imagine that you have never heard of Jesus Christ or Christianity. What do you think your reaction would be to what God has done in this passage? Explain your reaction.

4. Paraphrase verses 9-11.

How does God see us once we accept Christ's death and resurrection as the cure for our sins?

(We are no longer enemies of God. We need not be condemned because we are now reconciled to Him.)

5. What qualities of God are shown in Romans 5:6-11?

(We see God's love in sending us His Son and His mercy in forgiving us for our sins. He disciplines us because we need it, but He also shows mercy.)

6. Read Psalm 103:11. Now write down a description of God's correction based on this passage and what you've learned so far in this session.

Kids should point out that God corrects us for our sins to show us that we cannot get away with unrighteousness. God, in His perfection, does not tolerate wrong. At the same time, God shows compassion or mercy by providing a way of salvation for humans.

3 GROW WITH THE FLOW

Goal: That your students will complete a spiritual growth flowchart to identify areas where they may need God's correction.

Looking back over what we've just studied, how bad do you think people must be to be considered sinners?

(One sin separates us from God.)

Isn't it unjust for God to keep good people from salvation as He does the really bad people?

(Paul Little explained the Biblical teaching on this in *How to Give Away Your Faith* [InterVarsity Press, 1979]. He compared the human race to a group of swimmers who jump into the Pacific Ocean and start swimming toward Hawaii. The most moral person might make it 75 miles toward Hawaii. Perhaps the worst offender makes it 150 yards before he drowns. The rest of the human race is spread out between these two extremes. But what difference does it make how "good" someone is? Even the most moral person falls hundreds of miles short! Everybody will drown because nobody can swim that far. No matter how good we are by our own efforts, we fall far short of meeting God's standard of perfection.)

How good must we become before God offers us salvation?

(It is not our goodness that opens the door to God's mercy. It is our admission of guilt and sin. God provided a way to restore our fellowship with Him *because of* our wickedness.)

Christ's death and resurrection were the biggest things God did to correct mankind's sinful condition.

But God is still interested in all the specifics of our daily lives, even after we accept His salvation.

His correction is for our own well-being. He wants to shape us into spiritually stronger people, more pleasing to Him.

Have kids begin to apply this truth to their own lives by working on the "Spiritual Growth" flowchart (Action Sheet 13B). Be sure to go through the flowchart yourself ahead of time so that you can easily explain the instructions.

The following instructions will help you as you go over the chart with your kids.

Point A

Ask kids to jot down three "real-life" decisions in which they have needed God's correction in the past. These should be decisions which they might face again next week. Examples: What to do about a bad temper; what to do about a friend who let them down.

After that, kids should write some "potential conflicts" that might arise if they choose to follow God's principle in their decision.

Point B

As kids move to point B, they are following the path of Adam and Eve and of the people Paul talks about who turned toward ungodliness. When a person decides to rebel in his decision, then he is in need of correction. Kids should be able to fill in more examples of the results of choosing to ignore God's correction.

Point C

This point shows the good results of choosing to accept God's correction. Have kids rank the items here according to each item's importance to them.

Point D

Kids should now follow the arrows from point C to point D, going through "admit guilt to God" and "accept God's forgiveness." At point D, your kids should list positive values which come as a result of God's correction.

Spiritual Growth

The final outcome of this chart is spiritual growth. Kids should see that accepting God's correction turns out to benefit them.

Close your class in prayer. Ask kids to pray about the real-life decisions they wrote on their charts. Kids might also pray for the wisdom and strength to obey. Those who want to could thank God for His willingness to correct them when they disobey Him.

Encourage your kids to take their charts home to help them consider further how God works in their lives to correct them, leading them to spiritual growth.

Know God or No God?

Read these statements and find several ways to reply to them.

A. A Soviet cosmonaut claimed that on his trip into space he could not see God; therefore, God must not exist.

B. I can't accept the existence of God on faith. Faith is unscientific.

C. It's only a matter of time until people know all the answers. Scientists will eventually explain the universe without having to give God any credit.

GOD IS!

A Bible study on Genesis 1:1; Exodus 3:13-15;
Romans 1:19, 20; Hebrews 11:3.

1. Begin today's study by going through all the passages listed above as if you didn't know anything except what these Scriptures tell you about God. Then list all His characteristics which you can know for certain or which are implied in these verses.

Circle those on your list that are specifically stated, and be prepared to tell why you included the others. For example, in Genesis 1:1, you could circle the fact that God is the Creator.

You might also put on your list that He is eternal because this is implied. You can assume that if God was present in the beginning, He Himself had no beginning.

2. Reread Romans 1:19, 20. Below write a brief note to an imaginary or real friend, explaining how God can be seen through creation.

3. Think back over the Scriptures you've studied today. What verse would be the best evidence to give someone who refuses to believe there is a God? Explain your choice to one other person in the room.

4. Roleplay one of the following:

A. How would a Christian use the Scripture studied today and all the other information he or she knows to explain God's existence to a friend who doesn't believe that God exists?

B. A friend tells a Christian that he or she might have believed in God before we began to conquer space. But now humans have done so many things that people used to think only God could do. So the friend refuses to believe that there is a God.

Our Three-in-One God

Can God be three persons and be one God at the same time? Take a look at this sheet, and see what the Bible has to say.

I. One God

Israel was surrounded by pagan nations who believed in a lot of gods. These nations were always tempting the people of Israel to follow these gods. What does Moses say in Deuteronomy 6:4, 5 to counteract the temptation to worship many gods?

"Hear, O Israel: The Lord our God, the Lord is one. Love the Lord your God with all your heart and with all your soul and with all your strength" (Deut. 6:4, 5).

Why does verse 5 naturally follow, if verse 4 is true?

How do you think God's oneness separates Him from the "other gods" of this world?

How does Isaiah 43:10b, 11 support this view?

"Before me no god was formed, nor will there be one after me. I, even I, am the Lord, and apart from me there is no savior" (Isaiah 43:10b, 11).

Explain how each of the following references supports the idea of the Trinity:

Hebrews 1:3

John 1:1

John 5:23

John 14:8, 9

John 14:26

Philippians 2:5, 6, 9, 10

Acts 5:3, 4

Matthew 28:19

II Corinthians 3:17

II Corinthians 13:14

II. Three-in-One

Suppose you had to describe the idea of the Trinity to a friend at school who had never heard of it before. What would you say?

Like God Or Not?

Take a look at the following comparisons which are sometimes used to explain the Trinity. Fill in the chart with your thoughts on how the subject of each analogy is like God or not like God.

Analogy	How is it like God?	How is it not like God?
A musical chord played on piano or guitar.		
A basketball team during a game.		
A car engine.		
The three sides of a triangle.		

Our Fatherly God

ACTION SHEET 3A

*God is our Heavenly Father. That's nothing new to you, right?
But what does it really mean? As you go over the following
study, you'll find out!*

1. We sometimes refer to God the Father as the Creator. List three creative things He did according to Acts 17:24-28. Be specific.

Here is the passage: "The God who made the world and everything in it is the Lord of heaven and earth and does not live in temples built by hands. And he is not served by human hands, as if he needed anything, because he himself gives all men life and breath and everything else. From one man he made every nation of men, that they should inhabit the whole earth; and he determined the times set for them and the exact places where they should live. God did this so that men would seek him and perhaps reach out for him and find him, though he is not far from each one of us. 'For in him we live and move and have our being.' As some of your own poets have said, 'We are his offspring.' "

2. God created people, and in doing that He became the Father of everyone—Christians and non-Christians. But He is uniquely the Father of those who are living examples of Galatians 3:26. How would you explain that verse to someone who says to you, "God is everyone's Father. What's so special about Christians?"

Here is the verse: "You are all sons of God through faith in Christ Jesus."

3. Read Matthew 6:6-13; then fill out the following chart, using all of the Scriptures we've looked at so far in this session.

Here is the Matthew passage: "When you pray, go into your room, close the door and pray to your Father, who is unseen. Then your Father, who sees what is done in secret, will reward you. And when you pray, do not keep on babbling like pagans, for they think they will be heard because of their many words. Do not be like them, for your Father knows what you need before you ask him.

"This, then, is how you should pray:

" 'Our Father in heaven, hallowed be your name, your kingdom come, your will be done on earth as it is in heaven. Give us today our daily bread. Forgive us our debts, as we also have forgiven our debtors. And lead us not into temptation, but deliver us from the evil one.' "

What God Does for Us

What God Asks of Us

4. Read Matthew 7:11. How is God the Father similar to a good earthly father? How is He different? Summarize your answers to these two questions in two or three sentences.

Here is the verse: "If you, then, though you are evil, know how to give good gifts to your children, how much more will your Father in heaven give good gifts to those who ask him!"

If God Were Here

Bow down and worship	*Gain confidence against Satan*
Seek to live holy lives	*Feel the peace of God's love*
Try to love others more fully	*Feel the guilt of unconfessed sin*
Get excited about serving God	*Desire to remain with Him*
Develop a desire to learn from Him	*Realize how small we are*

Picture The Son

Use your creative abilities to express on this sheet what you know about Jesus.

1. Use words, lines, or symbols to describe God the Son as He is pictured in Hebrews 1:2, 3.

Which of the descriptive phrases in Hebrews 1:3 means the most to you right now? Why?

2. Use lines, words, or symbols to show the relationship between God the Father, God the Son, and the angels (Hebrews 1:4-8, and John 1:1-3). (The angel part is easy, but double-check the relationship between Father and Son.)

3. Read John 1:4-10. The Word is Jesus. With words, symbols, and stick figures, explain what is happening in these verses. To do this, you will have to identify what is meant by light and darkness.

4. Someone says Jesus was just a good man, a great teacher. Respond by completing the sentences:

A. Wrong, according to (insert verse from today's text) _____________ , Jesus is _____________ .

B. Wrong, according to (insert verse from today's text) _____________ , Jesus is _____________ .

C. Wrong, according to (insert verse from today's text) _____________ , Jesus is _____________ .

JESUS, THE ONE AND ONLY

What is so unique about the Jesus we read about in the Bible?

HIS INCREDIBLE AUTHORITY

Over disease, death, nature, demons, sin, circumstances, and the future.

HIS ASTONISHING WISDOM

Nobody had ever talked the way Jesus did. See Matthew 7:28; 13:54; Mark 11:18.

HIS SERVANT ATTITUDE

Jesus was a suffering Servant. He was self-assured, confrontive, commanding. But He was like a servant in that He never let His position isolate Him from the needs of others. He served humankind.

HIS PERFECT LOVE

He had compassion toward everyone—even those the world considered unimportant; even those who wanted to kill Him. His love was given quickly and generously, and often with nothing expected in return.

HIS POWERFUL RESURRECTION

Christ said He would rise from the dead, and He did! His resurrection was overwhelming, incredible, powerful, delightful—the mark of God's involvement and the basis of our hope.

HIS FUTURE RETURN

Jesus will return to earth in victory one day. He'll take us to live with Him forever. The Gospels emphasize this teaching, and the writers of other New Testament books underscore it. Jesus *will* come back!

The Parable of the Wireless Wonder

ACTION SHEET 5A

by Karen Burton Mains

After years of research, James Pheeney McBean thought he had invented the answer to correct all of the world's moral problems—The Wizard Wireless Wonder.

Volunteers from Central High School agreed to wear computer-activated sensors for a day. These sensors would react to slight rises in body temperatures and put the Wonder to the test. At last, all systems were go.

"Gentlemen," McBean addressed the gathered press, "I have discovered that a slight, but significant, rise in body temperature occurs whenever humans contemplate evil. Whenever one of our volunteers thinks about cheating on an exam or lying about overdue assignments, the rise in body temperature will be monitored by sensors that will ring a small buzzer as a reminder not to do wrong.

"At the end of this day, the waiting world will know if we have a cure for its ills."

But when the test ended, James Pheeney McBean discovered he still had some bugs in his invention.

One volunteer complained, "My buzzer went off 17 times in one class period! I was mortified!"

"Gentlemen," said McBean to the press, "the concept behind my invention is valid. However, I am going to start working on a way to make the buzzer audible only to the wearer. An ear implant maybe. I'll call you again when I get it perfected."

Poor McBean. The Christian already has an inner buzzer that warns of evil. It is supernaturally activated—by the Holy Spirit.

Spirit Search

Search through John 14:15-21 and use these questions to find out all you can about the Holy Spirit.

1. In verse 16, what name did Jesus give the Holy Spirit? How does the name describe His function?

The Greek word translated "Comforter" might better be translated "Helper." The word might literally be translated "one called alongside." The idea is that of one being there to help when needed.

2. What does it mean to us that Jesus promised "one called alongside"?

3. Jesus commanded something before He promised the Holy Spirit. What was that command?

4. Why do you think Christ referred to the Comforter as the Spirit of Truth?

5. What does the word "comfortless" (vs. 18) mean?

6. What event was Jesus talking about when He used the phrase "little while" (vs. 19)?

7. Verse 19 indicates that believers will see Jesus. Since He is in Heaven, how does Jesus show Himself to His followers today?

INVESTIGATION ASSIGNMENTS

We're expanding our Spirit search! Each investigative team has an assignment to complete. Once all our assignments have been completed, we can put together a report on who the Holy Spirit really is.

TEAM X ASSIGNMENT
Here are your questions. Use the Scriptures below (or any other ones you can find) and search out the most accurate and complete answers you can.

Where does the Holy Spirit come from? What part does He play in the Christian's life? What are some of the things He does? Make a list of as many things as you can find.

Scriptures to check: John 14:15-21; 15:26; 20:21, 22; Hebrews 9:14; Romans 8:9, 14-16; Galatians 5:22, 23; I Corinthians 6:19; 12:7, 11; Titus 3:5.

We're expanding our Spirit search! Each investigative team has an assignment to complete. Once all our assignments have been completed, we can put together a report on who the Holy Spirit really is.

TEAM Y ASSIGNMENT
Here are your questions. Use the Scriptures below (or any other ones you can find) and search out the most accurate and complete answers you can.

What was the difference in the function of the Holy Spirit in the Old Testament and the New Testament? List some of the special things He did in the Old Testament.

Scriptures to check: John 7:39; Genesis 1:2; Job 33:4; Judges 3:10; 14:6; Exodus 31:3; I Samuel 16:13; Nehemiah 9:20.

We're expanding our Spirit search! Each investigative team has an assignment to complete. Once all our assignments have been completed, we can put together a report on who the Holy Spirit really is.

TEAM Z ASSIGNMENT
Here are your questions. Use the Scriptures below (or any other ones you can find) and search out the most accurate and complete answers you can.
What can you find out about the personality of the Holy Spirit? What is He like? List as many qualities as you can.

Scriptures to check: I Corinthians 2:11, 12; 12:11; Romans 8:4, 14, 16, 26, 27; 15:30; Galatians 4:6; Ephesians 4:30; Psalm 139:7-10; Isaiah 11:2; John 14:15-21; 20:21, 22.

A Conversation Overheard

Look, no religious hocus-pocus for me. No blind faith. No emotion. Just cold, hard facts.

Everything proved by the scientific method, right?

Right! Experimentation and observation. Seeing is believing, I always say. And I never just assume that anything is true.

What about something like love? You can't prove it scientifically, but it's still there.

I've heard that one before. But love is something very different from the questions that science can answer.

Then you admit that there are some questions that science can't answer?

Okay, I admit it. But evolution is different. There's evidence for it.

Evidence that humans came from the ape?

Something like that.

And that apes came from fish?

Well, that's a simple way to put it, but true.

And that the fish came from one-celled animals?

Right.

Where did the one-celled animals come from?

Chemicals on the earth combined to form life.

Where did the chemicals come from?

They were here on the earth. And to answer your next question, the earth and the whole universe probably came from the explosion of an incredibly dense piece of matter floating in the middle of nothing.

Okay, where did the piece of matter come from?

Well, it was just there. We have to assume. . .

But you said that you never assume anything that can't be proved scientifically.

Look, why are you so interested in this thing, anyway?

You were supposed to have the answers. Maybe "Where did it all come from?" is one of the questions that science can't answer.

How about changing the subject? Okay?

What's So Special About People?

Push your mind back in time to the very beginning—to the awesome time when "In the beginning God created the heavens and the earth" (Genesis 1:1). God created a universe so huge we can't find the end of it, suns, moons, plants, animals, and finally humans. God said, "Let us make man in our image, in our likeness . . . . So God created man in his own image . . . male and female he created them" (Genesis 1:26, 27).

1. Look up Acts 17:26. What does this section from one of Paul's sermons tell you about creation?

Humans are special in God's creation. He "formed" man and woman instead of just calling them into existence like everything else in creation. And He formed us in His image!

Only people can reason. Only people have a conscience—a sense of right and wrong. This means we have the tremendous opportunity of knowing and loving God! Sure, our bodies resemble those of certain animals. We all had the same Designer! But our spirits, our souls, God made like Himself—to be able to do what is right, to reason, to be creative, to love Him, to be responsible to Him. You're made in God's image: you're special!

2. Why do you think the Bible doesn't tell us everything about creation, especially since so many people have such trouble believing it?

3. Since all people are made in the image of God, how do you think you should feel about yourself?

4. How should you think about others?

5. If we believe that people are unique, the highest level of God's creation, what difference does it make?

6. What might an evolutionist say is the purpose of man?

7. What does the Creation story tell us about the purpose of man?

GOD POWER

1. You and your friend have just seen a film on the marvels of science. Your friend turns to you and says, "The laws of science seem to point to the fact that the world can run itself without God. Therefore, God must not exist." How would you respond? Read the two passages below and come up with a response based on each.

Job 38:1-11

Genesis 1:14-18

2. According to the laws that God set up, the sun, moon, and stars all have a specific purpose. What is their purpose according to the Genesis passage you just read? Look also at Psalm 104:19-24.

3. In writing to the Colossians about Jesus Christ, the apostle Paul talks about an even bigger purpose for all the things of nature. Explain what this purpose is by putting Colossians 1:16, 17 into your own words.

4. These verses tell us that God made both the seen and the unseen. What are some of the unseen things?

5. How might these verses from Colossians help someone who's afraid that everything is falling apart and that God no longer has any power in the world?

6. How could you use Ephesians 3:20 and Philippians 4:13 to support the answers you gave above?

"ALL I HAVE SEEN TEACHES ME TO TRUST THE CREATOR FOR ALL I HAVE NOT SEEN."

—Ralph Waldo Emerson

WHAT IF . . .

> ## And the Lord God formed man . . . and he became a living being.

Suppose this statement were plastered in huge letters on a billboard beside a busy highway. What kinds of reactions would people have as they drove by and saw it?

Reactions:

WHY ARE WE HERE?

ACTION SHEET 8B

God created us. We know that. But why did He create us? Let's look at some Scripture to find out.

1. Read Genesis 1:26-28. In the space below, draw a diagram using symbols, lines, and words which illustrates the most important thing you learn in this passage about our relationship with God.

2. The fact that God created us in His own image suggests that God created us like Him so that we could relate to Him in some way. Read Ephesians 1:3-5. What kind of relationship did God have in mind when He created people?

3. Although humans were created in God's image, they have since fallen away into sin. Read Romans 1:21-23; Ephesians 2:1-3; Colossians 1:21. In what ways has sin spoiled our fellowship with God?

4. How can we be sure that God continues to reach out to us in love even though we have spoiled our relationship with Him through sin?

5. How does Acts 17:24-27 provide further evidence that God continues to seek fellowship with us?

6. God's purpose in creating us was that we might have fellowship with Him. Why do you think the God of all the universe was interested in fellowship with us? Read Jeremiah 31:3 and find out.

STATE YOUR CASE

Fill in the data below, first on God the Judge and then on the guilty person. Base any observations or conclusions on the evidence from Scripture.

1. The Judge

A. How do the following verses illustrate to you that God is just and is determined to seek justice?

Genesis 6:5-7

Romans 3:23-26

Psalm 98:8, 9

Revelation 6:17

B. How do the following verses illustrate to you that God is merciful?

Genesis 6:8, 9

Romans 3:23-26; 5:8, 9

2. The Client

A. What's the person's crime? Look at Genesis 6:5-7; Romans 1:21, 32; 3:10-12, 20, 23.

B. What if the person says, "I didn't know any better"? What kind of answer could you give him or her? See Romans 1:19, 20.

3. Conclusions

A. Assume this person is brought to trial. As you see what kind of judge God is and as you look over the person's case, what verdict do you think is possible? Explain.

B. Suppose the person signs into the court record his or her testimony that he or she is personally committed to the truth of Romans 3:23, 24. How does this affect the verdict?

C. How does this demonstrate the importance of God's mercy?

D. If you had to come before the Judge with your own case, which verdict would you receive? On what basis would you plead for mercy?

Sin

An inborn warp which makes us miss God's goal. When we sin, we stray off God's path and become separated from Him. We disobey God's instructions. We fail to grow more Christlike; we fail to become the whole people that God intended.

Justice

God, who is perfectly good and fair, has the responsibility of punishing evil in the world He has made. His justice is balanced by His love. By sending His Son to take the punishment for sin, He provided a way that people can be set right with Him.

Mercy

In His compassion, God chooses not to punish us even though we deserve to be punished. Through Christ Jesus He forgives us as we believe in Him.

Grace

Grace is the favor and help God gives us even though we have not earned it. God freely and lovingly gives us all we need to live as He plans both now and forever.

God Is . . .

Use the following Scripture texts to create a list of characteristics that describe what God is like. Some characteristics will be obvious from the text; others you can assume based on what the text tells you about God. Underline the attributes that were true at the time the Scripture was written and are still true of God today.

1. Malachi 3:6

"I the Lord do not change. So you, O descendants of Jacob, are not destroyed."

2. Exodus 20:1-3

"And God spoke all these words: 'I am the Lord your God, who brought you out of Egypt, out of the land of slavery.

"You shall have no other gods before me.' "

3. Psalm 99: 2-5

"Great is the Lord in Zion; he is exalted over all the nations. Let them praise your great and awesome name—he is holy. The King is mighty, he loves justice—you have established equity; in Jacob you have done what is just and right. Exalt the Lord our God and worship at his footstool; he is holy."

Based on the words you've underlined, make one observation about God.

*G*ive me a hundred men who will hate sin and nothing else, and fear God and nothing else, and I will change the world.

—John Wesley

No Laughing Matter

Ever promise someone you would swim oceans for her or slay a purple dragon in his honor? Naturally the person you made the promise to didn't hold his breath because he knew that what you had promised went against natural laws. No matter how often you practiced swimming across the city pool, you wouldn't build up the strength to make it to Tokyo. And purple dragons are hard to find these days.

But suppose God made a promise that went against natural laws? Not a silly promise like those in our examples, but a serious and wonderful—and impossible-by-human-standards—promise.

That's what He did to Abraham and Sarah. He promised He would make a great nation from their children (Genesis 13:16). But they had no child!

Time passed and nothing happened. Things were becoming a little panicky since Sarah wasn't getting any younger.

In fact she was beyond the age when women became mothers. She was 75! Maybe Abraham and Sarah thought God didn't realize this human fact, so they decided to help Him out. Sarah suggested that her husband have a baby by one of her Egyptian servants. He did, and the bouncing boy was Ishmael.

But Ishmael wasn't the son God had promised. Abraham and Sarah should have realized that if God made natural laws, He could also do away with them when it suited His purpose.

About 14 years later, today's Scripture takes place. Three angelic visitors came to see Abraham. As they were leaving, one of them—the Lord Himself appearing in visible form—promised Abraham that He would give them a son in a year.

Giggle! Snicker! Laugh!

The seemingly utter impossibility of the whole thing caused Sarah, eavesdropping behind the tent door, to laugh to herself. God heard, and spoke some of the greatest words in the Old Testament: "Is anything too hard for the Lord?"

A year later Sarah was laughing again. This time it was with joy because God had kept His promise. The old couple had had a son! They named him Isaac, which comes from the Hebrew word for laughter.

Abraham and Sarah must have laughed many times as they enjoyed their son and remembered their foolish doubts about what God could and could not do!

Finders Keepers

Find the promises God makes in the following verses and put a check beside those which have already come true. How do you know the others will also come true?

Genesis 3:15
John 14:26, 28
John 15:10
I John 2:25
John 14:2, 3

Practicing The Promises

The Promise	What God Promises	My Part
Romans 10:9		
I John 1:9		
Matthew 21:22		
Exodus 20:12		
Revelation 2:10		
I John 3:22		

'ME?'

I mean, the universe is such a big place that our earth is a mere fly spot in space.

I have created you.

And with all the billions of people crowding our planet, I'm no more significant than a grain of sand on one of the ocean's beaches.

You are My child.

And with all the people who've lived in the centuries before me. . .

I have known you since before the day of your birth.

And all the people who'll live in the years after I'm gone. . .

You are precious to Me.

How could God possibly have time to give me any attention? Or even notice me? He probably doesn't even know I exist!

I have created you and you are My child. You are as important to Me as anyone who has ever lived.

Me? Are you talking about me? Are you sure?

DETAILS! DETAILS!

1. Read Genesis 1:11, 12, 24, 25. What characteristics or attributes of God do you find suggested in this description of Creation? Call them out as you find them.

2. Now read Matthew 6:30-33. What feelings do you think people were having that prompted Jesus to say this?

3. How would knowing the answer to question 1 help eliminate some of the anxieties the people were feeling in question 2?

4. The actions of many people in the Bible made it clear that they understood and believed the truth Jesus stated in Matthew. Look up the following references and tell how these people showed their faith that God could take care of details in their lives.

   A. *II Kings 4:1-7*

   B. *Mark 5:25-34*

   C. *Acts 7:57-60*
   Note: Stephen had just finished going through the history of the Jewish people in an effort to show the Jewish council that Jesus Christ was the Messiah.

5. Think of a person you know who lives as if he or she understands and believes the truth Jesus stated in the Matthew verses. List several ways he or she has shown faith that God could take care of the details of his or her life.

Task Calendar

Tasks:

Mon.	Tue.	Wed.	Thur.	Fri.	Sat.

How God Helped:

Mon.	Tue.	Wed.	Thur.	Fri.	Sat.

Lord, Will I Ever Learn?

LORD, WILL I EVER LEARN?
by Ruth Harms Calkin

You saw the whole thing, Lord.
Congested traffic
Me on my bike
Too much exhaust smoke
Nerves jarring.
You know how he infuriated me
Selfish driver
Egotistical.

He insisted on going around me, Lord.
Recklessly cutting in
Stopping short
Carelessly oblivious.
Then at a signal I watched it happen:
Sputtering motor
Steam billowing
Radiator spewing antifreeze
Stymied driver.

With forced control
Plus an open smirk
(Sorry, Lord)
I pedaled past him.
Almost home
Spontaneous relief.

Then just as I turned the corner
Your voice again:
I am
Much more patient
With you.

Adapted from Tell Me Again, Lord, I Forget *by Ruth Harms Calkin. Published by Tyndale House Publishers, Inc. © 1974. Used by permission.*

- -

Correction!

God's correction of humans is sometimes necessary. Let's see how He goes about correcting people who have done wrong.

1. When Adam and Eve ate the fruit from the forbidden tree, they disobeyed God and deserved to be punished.

   In Genesis 3 we have a vivid picture of how God goes about punishing or "correcting" those who have sinned against Him.

   A question comes up: What qualities does God exhibit in the process of correcting His people?

   Read through the references below and answer the question above for each reference.

   A. Genesis 3:8-13

   B. Genesis 3:14, 15

   C. Genesis 3:16-19

   D. Genesis 3:21

   E. Genesis 3:22-24

2. Writing in Romans, Paul adds to the picture we have of God. From what Paul says, why do you think it was necessary for God to "correct" humans for their sins? See Romans 1:18, 21-23; 5:12.

3. Read Romans 5:6-11. Imagine that you have never heard of Jesus Christ or Christianity. What do you think your reaction would be to what God has done in this passage? Explain your reaction.

4. Paraphrase verses 9-11.

5. What qualities of God are shown in Romans 5:6-11?

6. Read Psalm 103:11. On the back of this sheet, write a description of God's correction based on this passage and what you've learned in this session.

SPIRITUAL GROWTH FLOWCHART

ACTION SHEET 13B

REAL-LIFE DECISIONS (List Three)

Instructions: Begin at point A. Read and follow the arrow around to point B. (Or note how you can move directly from point A to SPIRITUAL GROWTH.) Study the choices at point B and keep following points C, D, and E on the arrow until you reach SPIRITUAL GROWTH. Fill in boxes as you go along. Rank the items listed under C in the order that they motivate you. What can this teach you about SPIRITUAL GROWTH?

CHOOSE TO OBEY GOD'S PRINCIPLE

CHOOSE TO REBEL

Develop Positive Values, Actualize God's Power, Experience the Abundant Life

POSITIVE VALUES (List a Few)

A LEADS TO... **D**

SPIRITUAL GROWTH

Experience Guilt,

God's Discipline,

Logical Consequences of Action

POTENTIAL CONFLICTS (List a Few)

1.

2.

ACCEPT GOD'S FORGIVENESS

Progress Toward the Image of JESUS CHRIST!

ADMIT GUILT TO GOD

B

CHOOSE TO ACCEPT GOD'S CORRECTION

BEGIN TO APPRECIATE GOD'S MOTIVES FOR CORRECTION:
You Receive Endurance
You Are Loved As a Legitimate Child
You Develop Respect for God
It Is Good for You
You Share God's Holiness
You Are Trained to Live the Right Way
You Receive Peace

(Hebrews 12:4-11)

C

CHOOSE TO IGNORE GUILT

Become Bitter Toward Authority

Rationalize Past Actions

Develop Negative Values

Other (List):